WEDNESDAY, FEBRUARY 11, 19

BRISTOL-LONDON BUS

Although not a good copy, this photograph from a local Marlborough paper was published just one day after Bristol Greyhound started its pioneering long distance service between Bristol and London, and the caption that accompanied it reflected upon the uniqueness of the occasion. It read "The oldest inhabitant of Chippenham, Wilts., remembers the novelty of trains in the early years of railways, but was astonished yesterday when told that a daily service of motor omnibuses between Bristol and London had been organised."

PRESS, BRISTOL, MONDAY, FEBRUARY 9, 1925.

The "GREYHOUND" MOTORS Ltd.

DAILY SERVICE
BETWEEN
BRISTOL & LONDON
By LUXURIOUS MOTOR SALOON COACHES,
Commencing February 11, 1925.

TIME TABLE (SUNDAYS INCLUDED)

	a.m.			a.m.
Bristol, Prince Street	Dep. 9.0	Hammersmith, Broadway	Dep.	9.0
Keynsham, Church	,, 9.30	Brentford, Magistrates' Court	,,	9.20
Saltford	,, 9.40	Hounslow, Broadway	,,	9.30
Newton St. Loe	,, 9.45	Slough, Crown Hotel	,,	10.10
Bath, Top Milsom Street	,, 10.0	Maidenhead, Bear Hotel	,,	10.30
Chippenham, Market Place	,, 10.50	Twyford	,,	10.55
Calne, Market Place	,, 11.15	Reading, London-Wokingham Rd.	,,	11.15
Beckhampton	,, 11.40	Newbury, Broadway	Arr.	12.15
Marlborough, Town Hall	,, 12.10	,, ,,	Dep.	12.45
Hungerford, Bear Hotel	,, 12.50	Hungerford, Bear Hotel	,,	1.10
Newbury, Broadway	Arr. 1.15	Marlborough, Town Hall	,,	1.50
,, ,,	Dep. 1.45	Beckhampton	,,	2.20
Reading, London-Wokingham Rd.	,, 2.45	Calne, Market Place	,,	2.45
Twyford	,, 3.5	Chippenham, Market Place	,,	3.10
Maidenhead, Bear Hotel	,, 3.30	Bath, Top Milsom Street	,,	4.0
Slough, Crown Hotel	,, 3.50	Newton St. Loe	,,	4.15
Hounslow, Broadway	,, 4.30	Saltford	,,	4.20
Brentford, Magistrates' Court	,, 4.40	Keynsham, Church	,,	4.30
Hammersmith, Broadway	Arr. 5.0	Bristol Prince Street	Arr.	5.0

FARES (EITHER WAY)

From \ To	Bath	Chippenham	Calne	Beckhampton	Marlborough	Hungerford	Newbury	Reading	Twyford	Maidenhead	Slough	Hounslow	Brentford	London, Hammersmith	RETURN FARE to London
Bristol	1/3	2/6	3/-	3/9	4/3	5/3	6/-	7/6	8/-	8/3	9/-	10/-	10/3	10/6	20/-
Bath	—	1/8	2/-	2/9	3/3	4/3	5/-	6/6	7/-	7/3	8/-	9/-	9/3	9/6	18/-
Chippenham		—	9d.	1/6	2/3	3/3	4/-	5/9	6/3	6/6	7/3	8/3	8/6	8/9	16/6
Calne			—	1/-	1/9	2/9	3/6	5/3	5/9	6/-	6/9	7/9	8/-	8/3	15/6
Beckhampton				—	1/-	2/-	2/9	4/6	5/-	5/6	6/-	7/-	7/3	7/6	14/6
Marlborough					—	1/3	2/-	3/9	4/3	4/6	5/3	6/3	6/6	6/9	13/-
Hungerford						—	1/-	2/9	3/6	3/9	4/6	5/6	5/9	6/-	11/6
Newbury							—	2/-	2/9	3/-	3/9	4/9	5/-	5/6	10/6
Reading								—	6d.	1/-	1/9	2/9	3/3	3/6	6/6
Twyford									—	9d.	1/6	2/3	2/9	3/-	5/6
Maidenhead										—	9d.	1/9	2/3	2/6	4/6
Slough											—	1/-	1/6	1/9	3/-
Hounslow												—	6d.	9d.	1/3
Brentford													—	6d.	1/-

Fares advertised on posters to Keynsham, Saltford, and Newton St. Loe have been cancelled in accordance with the Chief Constable's instructions.

LUGGAGE.
Small Suit Cases .... FREE.
Heavy or Bulky Luggage charged According to Weight or Size.

GREYHOUND MOTORS

The Story of a Long Distance Coaching Pioneer

GEOFF BRUCE
MIKE WALKER

Bristol Vintage Bus Group

Contents

	PAGE
• Early Days 1919 - 1925	1
• Long-distance services - expansion 1925 - 1928	12
• Takeover - under Bristol Tramways control 1928 - 1935	23
• Demise 1935, and Living - on in name 1936 - 1973	33
• Colour photographs	43

Appendices

1. Greyhound Motors fleet list..49
2. Charles Russet fleet list...55
3. Morning Star fleet list..57
4. Bristol Tramways and Bristol Omnibus vehicles in Greyhound liveries..58
5. Route data: bus services transferred to Bristol Tramways and Carriage Company..60
6. Map of routes..62
7. Organisation of Long Distance Coach Services (reprint of 1934 Omnibus Magazine article.)......................................68
8. Tickets..91
9. Timetables and leaflets..96
10. Extracts from Bristol Watch Committee Record Books, 1920 - 1930...107

Cover illustrations.
Front cover: Motor Coach tours brochure cover, circa 1930.
Inside front cover: Saloon Coach Service leaflet, 1933.
Inside rear cover: Bristol to London express coach service leaflet, 1967.
Rear cover: Greyhound Motors Ltd. Fleet logo.

Frontpiece illustrations.
Front: One of the first journeys on the Bristol to London express service, 1925.
Rear: Bristol to London express service, times and fares, 1925.

First published in 2010 by Bristol Vintage Bus Group (www.bvbg.org.uk), Unit H, Flowers Hill Industrial Estate, Brislington, Bristol, BS4 5LU.

Printed in Great Britain by St Andrews Press, St.Andrew's Park, Wells, Somerset, BA5 1TE.

© Geoff Bruce and Mike Walker 2010.

ISBN 978-0-9566267-0-7

All rights reserved. No parts of this publication may be reproduced, stored in a retrieval system, or transmitted in any form or by any means electronic, mechanical, photocopying, recording or otherwise, without prior permission of Bristol Vintage Bus Group.

Acknowledgements

Many people and organizations should be acknowledged as it has taken forty years of interest to bring these notes together. The trade magazines, The Commercial Motor, Motor Transport, The Booking Agents Journal, The Tramway & Railway World, Modern Transport, The Railway Gazette, The Transport World and possibly others. Newspaper reports consulted included the Reading Standard, and The Bristol Times & Mercury. I should also thank the officers and staff of Bristol City Council, The Bristol Records Office and Bristol Central Library where I consulted both Kelly's and Matthews directories. The Omnibus Society and P.S.V. Circle have been invaluable sources of information also. Various friends have also provided the benefit of their knowledge over the years including Mike Tozer, Allan Macfarlane, Alan Peters, Peter Davey, Martin Curtis, Dave Withers, Phil Sposito, Alan Janes, Mike Moggridge, Alan Neale, Brian Neil, Colin Martin, Roger Grimley, Bob Crawley, George Elliott and many others who have all contributed however unwittingly. Photographs have been made available from a number of collections, M. J. Tozer being the major source, who together with Peter Davey and The Bristol Vintage Bus group provided the majority.

Alan Neale is particularly thanked for providing many of the timetables illustrated, and Gerry Serpell-Morris is also thanked for the ticket collection. Mike Walker was instrumental in bringing all the various aspects together.

Mark Hughes is also thanked for his work on the local route map.

Geoff Bruce

Introduction

Why produce a book on the history of a bus company that disappeared in 1936? Lots of other bus companies have vanished and been forgotten – what was so different about Greyhound Motors of Bristol? Well, it was probably the first to incorporate the word "Greyhound" and to use a monogram of a dog of that pedigree: the Australian company of that name was formed in 1928 whilst the North American Company Greyhound Lines was formed in 1931.

There were other U.K. operators who used the word "Greyhound" in their titles in the 1920's (for example Greyhound Coaches, Weymouth) and in the post world war II era (Greyhound of Arbroath etc,) but these didn't endure, whereas the Bristol Greyhound lasted for nearly fifty years.

In late 2009 FirstGroup, who had some years earlier acquired the American Greyhound Company, re-introduced the name to Great Britain for its new express services, operating first between London and Southampton/Portsmouth – ironically all three places having been served by the original Greyhound Company. The symbolism is not lost there, however, as it could be claimed that FirstGroup, having been formed by the merger of two companies, one of which was Badgerline, which had in turn bought the Bristol Omnibus Company (previously Bristol Tramways and Carriage Company) from Midland Red (West), was the natural descendent of the original Greyhound Motors. However, FirstGroup, paid no heed to the historical significance of the return of the name to inter-city coach travel in the United Kingdom in its press launch of the new brand.

THE GREYHOUND MOTORS LIMITED

Early Days 1919 – 1925

Like many other charabanc operators, this company can be traced back to the end of the First World War, as so many men had been trained in the army to drive and to maintain motor vehicles, and also needed a job when they returned home; this seemed an opportunity not to be missed. Sydney J. Toogood and William T.Bennett started in business as timber merchants and haulage contractors. The Toogood family business was importing timber and selling timber products like garden sheds etc. and this was to continue for many years.

The lorries used were Dennis 3 ton or 4 tonners purchased as War Department surplus and by March 1920 several of these lorries were fitted with charabanc bodies built by messers F.G.Cox & Co. and Howard Stephens Ltd. for use on advertised trips to such places as Glastonbury and Wells, Minehead and Dunster, Bath, Bradford on Avon, Trowbridge, Freshford and Limpley Stoke etc. and for private hire, and very quickly a fleet of twenty such vehicles were put into use.

The original garage and office was at 40 Phillip Street, Bedminster but early in 1921 a larger garage was acquired in Trinity Street, St Philips, with an office just around the corner at 96 West Street, Old Market. The early livery was light grey with gold shaded block "GREYHOUND" fleet names along each side of the bonnet and fleet numbers (within a circle) on each side of the scuttle panels.

The majority of charabancs had prominent fleet numbers on both sides at the front and at the back, mainly it is believed to help passengers find "their" vehicle when some six or seven were in use on one trip. The "Greyhound" fleetname is displayed on the bonnet side. AE9710 is a 4 ton 40 horse power Dennis, with fleet number 1.
(M.J.Tozer collection)

The rear carried the title "GREYHOUND" again in gold shaded block lettering in an arched format at the top, with "MOTORS LIMITED", "96 WEST STREET" and "BRISTOL" in three lines of straight, shaded lettering below. The fleet number was repeated on each corner at the rear (again encircled). Each vehicle also carried its allocated hackney number on each side at the bottom of the front scuttle panel, in black lettering. (In spite of the photographer's best efforts to hide the identity of the vehicle) we are therefore usually able to identify most in old photos.

Greyhound's earliest charabancs were former war office "subsidy" chassis which were purchased as lorries, being of the 40 horse power type. Some of them were used as lorries by Greyhound before being rebodied as charabancs by Cox and Stephens of Bristol. AE8839 is a Dennis.

A rear view of No.4, HT1265, another Cox and Stephens bodied Dennis, shows the full details of the company's address. (M.J.Tozer collection).

The new charabanc venture proved very successful despite intense competition from many other operators including Bristol Tramways, and on 10th February 1921 a Limited Company "Greyhound Motors Limited" was registered with W. T. Bennett, F. White, A. E. Bryant (Traffic Manager), S. J. Toogood and William Palmer (secretary) as directors.

The next venture was to start local bus services. The first vehicles suitable for use as buses were purchased in 1921 for use on a route between St. Augustine's Parade (Tramways Centre) and Ashton Road (Tramway Terminal) via Victoria Street, Temple Meads, Bedminster Bridge, Coronation Road, Camden Road, Raleigh Road and Frayne Road, which was introduced on 23rd November 1921. The route was soon modified to go via Clift House Road and Ashton Avenue, and later extended via Winterstoke Road, Bedminster Down Road, Winford Road and Brunel Road to Bedminster Down.

This also proved to be a profitable venture and in 1922 four further City bus routes were started and nine buses were purchased, including four former Liverpool Tramways vehicles. The first of these new routes started on 8th February 1922 between Tramways Centre (Colston Avenue) and Fishponds (Cassell Road), via Rupert Street, The Horsefair, Milk Street, Lower Ashley Road, Warwick Road, Stapleton Road, Fishponds Road and Downend Road.

On the 12th April a service from Old Market Street (Careys Lane) to Eastville (Robertson Road) was started which proceeded, via West Street, Clarence Road, Easton Road, Devon Road and York Road. A route between Old Market and Filton Avenue via St Nicholas Road, Sussex Place, Sefton Park, Downend Road and Muller Road also started in 1922.

In May 1922 Greyhound were granted a licence to run from Colston Street to Kellaway Avenue, Horfield, at its junction with Cairns Road. With one vehicle, operating via Jamaica Street, Stokes Croft, Arley Hill, Redland Road and Coldharbour Road. This route was to have been extended back from Colston Street to the Joint Station (now Bristol Temple Meads Station), but the Watch Committee would not allow Greyhound to serve this part of the route.

Bristol City Council had received a number of complaints from local residents concerning the number of buses using what had been quiet suburban roads and resolved not to licence any more vehicles until this problem was resolved. It had the powers to curtail route licences as well as hackney licences for vehicles and therefore proposed that the maximum number of vehicles to be licensed for Greyhound local routes would be 15, with 1 spare, whilst the "Tramways" were to have 60 for City routes and 39 for country routes. Charles Russett had 3 for City routes, 1 for Bristol-Keynsham and 1 spare. As a matter of interest there were 144 charabancs also licensed at the time, 52 with Bristol Tramways, 13 with Greyhound, 4 with Russett and 75 others. The 3 main City route operators were requested by the Council to work out some way of reducing the number of vehicles in use.

In July 1922 the City council decided that the maximum number of standing passengers to be allowed on motor buses should be 4, although they deferred a decision on the standing capacity of the trams. In August, Greyhound started a fourth route, the starting point of which again was from Colston Avenue but this time running via Colston Street, Maudlin Street, Dighton St, Jamaica St, Cheltenham Road, Cromwell Road, North Road, Grenville Road, Belmont Road, Kent Road, Kennington Avenue, Ashley Down Road, Downend Road to Strathmore Road.

Bristol Hackney Records (appendix 1) show that 4-ton Dennis AE8311 was allocated to the Ashley Down route in 1923, when its body was finished.
(Peter Davey collection).

In November 1922 it was requested by the Watch Committee that all three stage operators increase their fares to just above the relevant tram fares. It was also announced that the Chief Constable could authorise the use of extra vehicles as required for special events.

At the meeting of December 1922 the Watch Committee issued the following statement:

"Licences for the following three months would be:-
Bristol Tramways: 47 City; 39 country; 9 spares
Greyhound Motors: 12 City; 3 spares
Charles Russett: 3 City; 1 country; 1 spare"

The committee further proposed that used ticket boxes be fitted to the City omnibuses.

On the December 23rd a communication was received by the Watch Committee from Bristol Tramways stating that they were not prepared to adhere to the various proposals, including the refusal of additional omnibus licences, and an appeal was to be presented through the Ministry of Transport.

Greyhound opened a new office at 5, St. Augustine's Place, adjacent to the Colston Street terminus and next door to the Bristol Tramways' head offices: in addition, a tours booking office was rented in nearby Colston Avenue. At this time all of Greyhound's activities were competing with Bristol Tramways in one way or another, be it trams, buses, tours or haulage.

On February 1st 1923 it was announced that an agreement had been reached between Greyhound and Bristol Tramways, following a meeting proposed by Greyhound directors Mr. A. E. Richards and Mr. S. Toogood on December 6th of the previous year. The following list of routes and vehicle allowances was published:

ROUTE	CO.	BUSES	FREQ
Colston St.- Avonmouth	BT	12	12
Colston St. - Kellaway Ave.	BT	2	2
Ashton Ave. - Sneyd Park	BT G	3 3	4
St. Johns Lane - Clyde Rd.	BT	6	4
Centre - Suspension Bdge.	BT	7	8

Route	Operator	FREQ	
Colston Ave. – Ashley Down (via Kent Rd.)	G	3	4
Colston Ave. – Ashley Down (via Cromwell rd)	BT	3	4
Colston Ave. – Cassell Rd.	BT G	3 3	6
Careys Lane – Thicket Avenue	BT CR	4 2	6
Careys Lane – Eastville	BT G	1 1	3
Careys Lane – Ashley Down	BT G	2 2	6
Careys Lane – St.Annes	BT CR	4 1	5

Code:
FREQ:-buses per hour
BT-Bristol Tramways
G – Greyhound
CR-Charles Russett

Mr C.F.Russett protested against these proposals and the following alterations were made, and the starting date was amended to 9th May 1923:

Avonmouth route, 10 buses, 10 buses per hour to North View, 5 buses per hour to Avonmouth.

Ashley Down via Kent Road, Bristol Tramways 2 buses, Greyhound 2 buses, 5 buses per hour.

Ashley Down via Cromwell Road, Bristol Tramways 3 buses, 3 buses per hour

Cassell Road route, Bristol Tramways 4 buses, Greyhound 4 buses, 8 buses per hour.

Careys Lane to Ashley down, Bristol Tramways 1 bus, Greyhound 2 buses, 4 buses per hour.

St. Annes route, 6 buses per hour. Bristol Tramways 4 buses, Charles Russett 1 bus.

On May 20th 1923 the charabanc operators were informed that they could no longer ply for hire in Colston Avenue and stands were made available in Queens Square and Anchor Road, with the Chief Constable being left to decide which side of Anchor Road was to be used.

On June 27th 1923 the Chief Constable informed the Watch Committee that a number of charabanc proprietors had taken offices in Colston Avenue and were not complying with the requirements of recent by-laws by advertising that their tours would commence from outside of these offices. He stated that this appeared to be directed at trying to defeat the provision of the law. In addition, on August 1st the Chief Constable reported that various omnibus proprietors with offices in Colston Avenue were not complying with the requirements of the by-laws and proposed to take action in the case of all infringements brought to his attention.

Greyhound applied for a route from Colston Avenue to St. Werburghs on October 16th 1923 but this was not allowed, and on the same date, jointly with Bristol Tramways, applied for a route to Portishead. The Watch Committee rejected this application on November 2nd.

At the Watch Committee meeting of December 13th Greyhound applied to use double deckers on its City routes but this was also not accepted. The Committee also made it known that they were not in favour of Sunday bus services and that operators would be persuaded to cut back on their Sunday workings!

Bristol Tramways and Greyhound were to appeal jointly to the Minister of Transport against the refusal of the Watch Committee to grant the Portishead service, and additionally Greyhound applied for a service to Clevedon, which was also not allowed, and Greyhound appealed to the Minister of Transport about this refusal on July 30th.

Also on July 30th, Bristol Tramways and Greyhound applied jointly to operate between Bristol and Portishead, using 2 buses each and operating every 45 minutes from Prince Street: the service was to be doubled on Bank Holiday and summer weekends. Despite previous practices, this was approved by the City council on July 30th. As a result of this success a further application was made to operate a similarly timed route to Clevedon on August 14th, but this was again refused. Notwithstanding these refusals, however, a number of further applications were made over the following months, and these are listed below:

DATE	ROUTE	DECISION
4.11.24	Colston Avenue-Staple Hill	Refused
4.11.24	Prince Street-Frome	Refused
4.11.24	Augmentation of Fishponds route	Refused
24.2.25	Colston Avenue-Fishponds and Kingswood	Unsuitable
24.2.25	Fishponds-Kingswood	Deferred
24.2.25	Eastville-Westbury-Coombe Dingle	Deferred
24.2.25	Prince Street-Cosham	Unsuitable
24.2.25	Colston Avenue-Southmead	Unsuitable

As the actual routes were not recorded, it is not possible to know which parts of the various routes were considered unsuitable.

The company was informed that as from February 16th 1925, for a period of one year, the Cumberland swing bridge would be closed to traffic and that any bus route using the bridge should be diverted to use Broad Quay, Prince Street and Prince Street bridge.

Several buses were purchased with or re-bodied with bodies of Strachan & Brown "Parlour Saloon" design, HU991 is another Dennis 4-ton chassis with 30 seats, seen at the Sneyd Park terminus of route A (see following chapter).
(Bristol Vintage Bus Group collection).

Fleet number 1 was allocated to AE9710, a Dennis 4-ton chassis with a Cox & Stephens 28-seat charabanc body. Greyhound's earliest charabancs were these former War Office "subsidy" chassis, purchased as lorries, and may well have been used as such by Greyhound before being bodied to carry passengers. (M.J.Tozer collection).

HT756 (number 3) and HT3521 (number 10), two more Cox & Stephens bodied Dennis charabancs, the former a 4-ton model seating 28, the latter a 3-ton model seating 27. (M.J.Tozer collection).

4-ton Dennis HT756, (number 3), clearly shows the fleetname on the bonnet side and the fleet number on the side of the scuttle. Compare this photograph with that of number 4, over, showing that the doors and steps were on the near side only. (M.J.Tozer collection).

Cox & Stephens bodied Dennis 4-tonner number 4, HT1265. (M.J.Tozer collection).

Two further views of number 4, HT1265, showing the nearside entrances and step, and the seating layout with the hood folded at the rear. (Alan Lambert).

(M.J.Tozer collection).

Cox and Stephens bodied Dennis 4-ton number 5, HT1266, acquired in 1920 and pictured at Romsey Abbey.
(M.J.Tozer collection).

A line up of Greyhound charabancs at Southampton: featured, amongst others, are HT3520, HT3519, HT2626 and HT1266, numbers 9, 2, 7 and 5 respectively. HT3520 is a 3 ton chassis, the others are 4 tonners. The date is July 2nd 1923, and the company carried 1000 passengers in 38 coaches for a tour of the liner "Majestic": it was reported that two mechanics were carried in case of emergency, but the only involuntary stop was a brief one to change a magneto!
(M.J.Tozer collection).

Two views of line-ups of Dennis charabancs, featuring types with off side steps in addition to the near side ones. (M.J.Tozer collection).

In About 1923 this small Daimler was bodied by Strachan and Brown to their "Parlour Saloon" type with sliding roof panels and 23 seats. It had been registered in about 1918 as AE8023, and as a lorry. (M.J.Tozer collection).

AE8023 appeared to have had solid wheel centres on all but the nearside rear, which had spokes. The use of the word "Reserved" rather than "Private" is interesting as its use was continued in Bristol Tramways and Bristol Omnibus days for the destination display for driver training buses. (Peter Davey collection).

T7174, number 8, was, apart from the ex-War Office chassis, the first charabanc to be purchased second hand. It was new to South Devon Garages of Torquay, who traded as "Grey Cars", and was acquired in June 1924, when pneumatic tyres were fitted. It retained its Grey Cars fleet number. (M.J.Tozer collection).

Long-Distance And Local Services/Expansion 1925 To 1928

Possibly due to Bristol Tramways rapid expansion of bus services in the area during this period Greyhound decided on working a route of a different kind.

On February 10th 1925 a stage service to London was started. The Bristol terminus was Prince Street, and the route proceeded via the A36 and A4 (which had been newly named as such a year earlier) with a multitude of listed stopping places the principle ones being: Keynsham, Bath, Chippenham, Newbury, Reading, Maidenhead and Slough terminating at 229 Hammersmith Road, Hammersmith, London. There were three daily departures from each end. At 9:00am, 11:00am and 4.00pm from Bristol and at 9:00am, 12:00 noon amd 4:00pm from Hammersmith. The 11:00am from Bristol was soon diverted to service Bath, Bradford-on-Avon, Trowbridge, Melksham and Devizes. Similarly the noon departure from London was diverted via Devizes, Melksham, Trowbridge, Bradford-on-Avon and Bath started on March 2nd 1926.

The through fare between Bristol and London was £1 with the minimum for one stage being 6d. (2 ½p). A small garage was obtained in Hammersmith to house two vehicles overnight. Greyhound was licensed with all the authorities along the route to pick up and set down passengers except for London. Passengers could be set down at the Clarendon Hotel, but passengers for the west had to book at least 15 minutes before departure, and could not be set down until outside of the metropolitan police area. The service was immediately very successful and up to six or seven duplicates were sometimes required rendering the small Hammersmith garage less than adequate. Initially a conductor was carried to collect fares at the Bristol end and he was expected to collect all the fares before reaching Brislington where he alighted and caught the tram back into town. This practice soon stopped however as it proved nigh impossible and thereafter conductors were carried all the way. The service coach conductor was expected to collect the fares on any duplicates even when charabancs were used and running boards were the only access to each row of seats.

Long distance coach travel was of course not new but the novel feature of Greyhound's route was that anyone could turn up on the day along the line of route to travel without pre-booking save for the London 15 minutes provision. Consequently this was considered to be the first true express service in the country.

The original vehicles used on this service were Dennis 2 ½ ton chassis running on Henley air cushion tyres (solids). The Strachan & Brown 24 seat bodywork was then considered very luxurious with its spring backed seats and drop windows.

Contemporary reports said that the Greyhound Motors venture must stand as one of the boldest made , for in this case the facilities offered were in direct competition with one of the best train services in the Kingdom. In those days the chance of success for a coach service of this kind was an unknown quantity.

Returning to local services, the traffic sub committee of the Watch Committee next met on March 24th 1925 and were resolved to grant the following Greyhound operations:

One licence for the Eastville to Durdham Downs route, joint with Bristol Tramways, operating via Napier Road, Stapleton Road, Dormer Road, Muller Road, Wellington Hill, Kellaway Avenue, Coldharbour Road, Iddisleigh Road, Durdham Park and Durdham Down (corner of Stoke Road).

Consideration of the application to operate a service from Fishponds to Kingswood was pending a report from the City engineer as to making the provision for foot passengers crossing the railway bridge at Fillwood Road, Fishponds.

There was also an account concerning the proposed London service:

The Town Clerk read a letter which he had written to the Ministry of Transport enquiring whether the Ministry had given their approval to a scale of fares submitted by Greyhound on January 27th for intermediate stops between Bristol and Bath, and submitted a reply to the effect that a decision by the Ministry was not required as Bath Corporation had agreed to reconsider the application made to them by the company, who they understood had agreed to a suggestion made by the Corporation of Bath that the first fare stage on the west side of Bath should be at Newton St. Loe and on the east side at Chippenham, with no intermediate fares.

On the same date, the sub-committee agreed to renew the licences in respect of the London service for a further period of one month subject to a written undertaking being given by the company:

... to entirely remove the seat in front of the emergency exit together with its supports and fittings from the omnibuses engaged on this route, and to give further written instructions that they would not charge intermediate fares between Bristol and Bath, and that between the two points the fare should be 1 shilling and 3 pence (6 ½ pence). This was revised by mutual agreement to one shilling in January 1927.

At about this time Bristol city Council tried to introduce a new by-law to have all omnibuses licensed for use in Bristol to be fitted with pneumatic tyres, but the Minister of Transport would not support such a move, saying that, in his opinion, such tyres were not essential for use on omnibuses.

On May 19th Greyhound suggested that they be allowed to run temporarily buses to Fishponds via Lodge Causeway, or as an alternative, to stop at the Kingswood end of Fillwood railway bridge until the widening of the bridge was completed. The Council agreed to this proposal and the required number of licences were issued. The Lodge Causeway bridge was eventually completed in July 1926.

On May 19th a new route was suggested to run between Hotwells and Westbury on Trym via Bridge Valley Road, but was refused, but an extension of the Sneyd Park and Ashton service to either Long Ashton (Cider Institute) or the Cross Hands at Bedminster Down was allowed in respect of the Bedminster Down section, and a similar concession was to be made to Bristol Tramways with whom the service was jointly operated.

Yet another route extension was sought, this time for the Fishponds route to go on to Mangotsfield, but as this was outside of the Bristol City boundary no action could be taken by the Council! This route was later extended beyond Mangotsfield to Chipping Sodbury.

A rather different matter concerned the parking of Bristol Tramways' vehicles on the road outside of the Greyhound offices at St. Augustine's Parade, which interfered with the conduct of the company's business. The Council replied that they could not be involved in the matter having regard to all of the circumstances.

Finally, the company wished to increase the Eastville to the Downs service during the forthcoming Whitsuntide, to which the Committee acceded, as long as other services were maintained in the normal way.

In August 1925 the Watch Committee (Traffic) Sub Committee resolved that new applications would only be accepted at meetings to be held at the beginning of March, June, September and December, and that operators should submit any applications before the first of these months.

Two more applications for route licences were submitted by Greyhound before the new conditions came into force. The first, to extend the Fishponds to Durdham Downs service via The Promenade (in Clifton) to the Suspension Bridge, giving a 15-minute service, was agreed. However, the decision on the request to divert the Kingswood to Fishponds route to run over Lodge Causeway bridge was to be deferred until the following December.

At that December meeting Greyhound received one extra licence for the extension to Careys Lane of the Ashley Down route, as did the "Tramways".

A licence for a route to Dundry was granted on February 17th 1925 with 2 vehicle licences, and an additional licence was issued for the London service.

Also at that meeting Greyhound asked to substitute two single deck licences and replace them with two licences for double deckers on the route to Cassell Road and Fishponds. This was permitted as long as the vehicles were new and were of the same type as existing double deck omnibuses, but it was not until 1926 that these entered service, as HU3524-6.

On February 3rd 1926 Greyhound applied to use covered top double deckers on the Sneyd Park and Bedminster services but the Watch Committee considered that this was not a suitable route due to the steep hills that were involved, but that they would not object to the vehicles being used on the Eastville to Downs route via Muller Road, providing that Greyhound undertook to carry out certain modifications to the vehicles to meet Watch Committee's recommendations. A demonstration vehicle had been shown to the chairman of the Watch Committee, and previously to the Chief Constable, hoping to get their approval: this was granted, but only on the condition that they ran on pneumatic tyres.

Application was made on March 29th 1926 for five more routes together with alterations to three others, although none of these were granted: however, additional "rush hour" buses were permitted on the Strathmore Road service.

On the London service, the alternative route via Devizes was furnished with two AEC 411 "Renown" coaches in March 1926, two similar vehicles being introduced onto the main service, replacing the two original Dennis coaches. The new vehicles were painted grey with black window surrounds and a dark blue line below the windows: all of the main side windows were of the full drop variety. A new Greyhound bulls-eye motif was featured on each side: these vehicles introduced pneumatic tyres to the fleet.

March 1926 saw the introduction of the four AEC 411s with Strachan and Brown 26-seat bodies to replace the solid tyred Dennis coaches on the London service: all four ran on pneumatics. Their livery was grey with black window surrounds and a dark blue waistrail, and featured the large "bulls-eye" Greyhound insignia on each side with a smaller image at the rear. HU4805 is seen here in London.
(Bristol Vintage Bus Group collection).

On June 17th 1926 Bristol Tramways and Greyhound jointly applied to operate a new service to Avonmouth via the newly constructed Portway. The sub committee were in favour of such a route but required a number of conditions to be met.

It was requested that through fares be available from the Tramways Centre by tram to Hotwells and then transferring to the bus on to Avonmouth. Bristol Tramways accepted this for its own buses, but would not entertain this for transfer to Greyhound buses. Passengers transferring to these buses would be required to pay a separate fare.

It was also directed that the Hotwells terminus was to be on the site of the old Port and Pier railway station, that all new omnibuses were to have pneumatic tyres, headlights were to be dimmed and windows on the riverside of the buses were to be screened at night (obviously different sides of the bus in different directions!) Double decker buses could be used but no trailers (!) were to be allowed! Finally, road signs were to be erected at both ends of the road asking drivers to use dimmed headlights at night, so as not to interfere with shipping navigation lights!

In the event Bristol Tramways were granted six licences and Greyhound two, and the service started in early July, with Bristol Tramways using "Bristol" 4-tonner buses and Greyhound using either Dennis G or AEC double deck NS buses. The "Tramways" gave the service the number 99 and Greyhound the letter K.

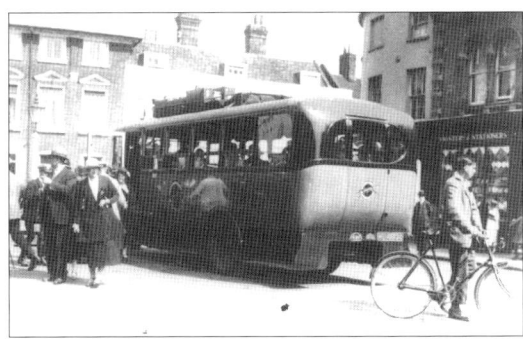

This rear view of similar coach HU4804 at Newbury shows the side and rear "Greyhound" insignia.
(M.J.Tozer collection).

Route letters were introduced by Greyhound at around this time and the August 1926 timetable listed the routes as follows:

A. Sneyd Park - Downs - Victoria Rooms - Tramways Centre - Victoria Street - Temple Meads - Bedminster Bridge - Dean Lane - East Street - Camden Road - Ashton Avenue - Bedminster Down (Tram terminus).

B. Colston Avenue - Jamaica Street - Stokes Croft - Cheltenham Road - Cromwell Road - Fry's Ground (now known as the County Cricket Ground) - Downend Road - Horfield (Downend Road rather than Strathmore Road).

C. Tramway Centre – Warwick Road - Eastville - End of Ridgeway Road - Fishponds (Cheapside later Vandyke) - Fishponds (Cassell Road).

D. Old Market - St Nicholas Road - Sussex Place - Sefton Park - Downend Road - Muller Road - Filton Avenue

E. Old Market (Carey's Lane) - Easton Road - Devon Road - York Road - Robertson Road (Eastville tram terminus).

F. Bristol (Prince Street) - Ashton Tram Terminus - Ashton Court Lodge - Beggar Bush Lane - Abbots Leigh (The George) - Haberfield Hill - Ham Green - Pill (Green) - Easton in Gordano (Kings Arms) - Portbury (The Priory) - Sheepway (Post Box) - Portishead (Albion Hotel) - Portishead (Battery Road) - Portishead (Golf House) - Portishead (Nautical School) - Portishead (Redcliffe Bay).

G. Eastville (Robertson Road) - Eastville (Park Gates, Muller Road) - Ashley Hill Station (footpath) - Muller Road Top (Wellington Hotel) - Coldharbour Road - Linden Road (end) - Redland Road - Durdham Downs - Stoke Road (Blackboy Hill top) - Zoological Gardens - Clifton Suspension Bridge - Clifton Rocks Railway (top).

H. Fishponds Station - Chester Park - Cossham Hospital - Soundwell Road - Kingswood Hotel - The Flower Pot Hotel (Kingswood).

J. Prince Street - Ashton Avenue (Swingbridge) - Ashton (tram terminal) - Bedminster Down (tram Terminal) - Bishopsworth (Elm Tree) - Dundry (The George).

K. Hotwells (tram terminal) - Portway (Sea Mills Bridge) - Portway (Sylvan Way) - Portway (Barrow Hill Road) - Avonmouth.

Notes

Route A was later extended to serve Cheddar Grove and terminated at Brunel Road.

Route E & G were later combined to run from Old Market to Clifton.

Route K was later extended into the city (Prince Street) from Hotwells via Cumberland Road and Wapping Road

Greyhound's first double deck bus, AEC 409 HU3524 with Short Brothers open staircase body took fleet number A11 after take over by B.T.& C.C.. Greyhound's coaches would have passed hundreds of identical "NS" buses every day on their journeys through the streets of London. (A.E.C.)

The introduction of double deckers was actually quite an event as buses with top decks had not been seen in Bristol since 1907 when Bristol Tramways original fleet of Thornycrofts were re-bodied to single deck, although, of course, Bristol's trams had always been double deckers. Three AEC "NS" 409 types with open top Short Brothers bodies and solid tyres arrived early in 1926 and used on route "C" and took registration numbers HU3524-3526. In April a similar vehicle, but with a covered top and pneumatic tyres, arrived, and was registered HU5150, followed by similar vehicle HU7240. Three further AEC "NS" also came in April, these had London General fleet numbers on their bonnet sides, NS2051-2053, but for unknown reasons these were returned to London five months later.

Three later AEC 409s were received with pneumatic tyres and top covers: they were delivered with London General fleet numbers NS2051/2/3, but only stayed with Greyhound for 5 months HU8159 is seen at the Hotwells end of the Avonmouth route 99 (later K).
(M.J.Tozer collection).

In December 1926 an application was made to Stroud Urban district Council to operate a Malmesbury-Tetbury-Stroud service on Tuesdays. The first application was refused but after further consideration a licence was granted on January 17th 1927 for two buses, one 28-seat and one 30-seat. Licences for buses IA4322 and HR5593 had been issued by Bristol City Council in respect of a Bristol to Malmesbury route, and so these buses were probably for this route through to Stroud.

A group of routes based on Malmesbury was started at this time:

Route "M" linked Sherston to Swindon (daily) via Easton Grey, Malmesbury and Brinkworth,

Route "N" was the Stroud-Tetbury-Malmesbury route mentioned above,

Route "P" was a Wednesday only route from Malmesbury to Bath via Sherston and Acton Turville, confirmed by the Bath Watch Committee on January 5th 1927.

Route "Q" was from Malmesbury to Bristol via Chipping Sodbury, operating on Thursday only,

Route "R" linked Malmesbury and Chippenham on Mondays and Fridays, 3 trips each day, via Luckington, Yatton Kennell and Allington.

Two further routes started in 1927:

Route "T" operated between Fishponds (Cassell Road) and Chipping Sodbury, daily: Cassell Road was the city boundary on the Staple Hill tram route,

Route "V" ran between Knowle and Bedminster Down.

In the meantime expansion of express services had started, two services between Bristol and Bournemouth being introduced in January 1927, one via Bath, Warminster, Salisbury and Ringwood, the other via Frome, Shaftesbury and Blandford Forum. Initially there was just one journey per day on each route, but very soon there were departures at 8.30 a.m. and 2.30 p.m. from Prince Street in Bristol for the route via Salisbury, arriving at Bournemouth (Richmond Garage, The Square) at 1.00 p.m. and 7.00 p.m. respectively. The route via Frome serving the same terminal points left at 9.00 a.m. and 4.00 p.m. arriving at 1.45 p.m. and 8.15 p.m. Departures from Bournemouth were at 8.45 a.m. and 2.00 p.m. on the route via Shaftesbury and 9.30 a.m. and 3.30 p.m. via Frome. The former route was later to be extended to Southsea, operating as a joint service with Olympic Motor Services of Southsea in April 1930.

Olympic's services passed to Travellers Saloon Coaches of Plymouth at the end of 1932 after that operator acquired the Olympic business, and subsequently Travellers Saloon Coaches was acquired by Elliot Brothers (Royal Blue) of Bournemouth in 1933.

In the summer of 1927 six new coaches were purchased for the London services and the trade press of the time seemed to have been quite taken with them as several magazines had full reports of the fleet of "Sumptuously Equipped Saloon Buses", to quote from the "Commercial Motor" of June 28th 1927. In fact only four of the six new coaches were so equipped two of them having 32 seats in the "orthodox" layout. It is interesting to note that similar reports in "Motor Transport" quote the seating as 18 in the front section and 8 in the smoking saloon.

"The chassis, which serves as the basis of the vehicle is the Associated Daimler 416A which is equipped with a 35-40 hp poppet valve engine. It has a frame height of only 2ft and being shod with pneumatic tyres of 38 inches by 7 inches dimensions and having four-wheel brakes it is an ideal vehicle for passenger services, particularly as it is fast and silent in operation.

The high-class type of body which is used is the product of Strachan & Brown, Wales Farm Road, London W3 and it provides seating and accommodation for 26 people. It is divided into three distinct sections. The foremost compartment is for 20 people arranged in the orthodox manner, that is to say each transverse seat for two people is disposed on each side of a central gangway. Then there is a central section on one side of which is a lavatory and on the other a small buffet. The rear portion, which is designed as a smoking compartment seats six people and is arranged on sociable lines."

HU9640 is one of the 4 ADC 416A vehicles with Strachan and Brown 26seat coach body: the fleet number became A106 when the bus passed to Bristol Tramways.
(Peter Davey collection).

In November 1927 Greyhound made an application to extend service "D" to the "Duke of York" on Horfield Common pending the extension of Filton Avenue, which was being built at that time: the council deferred the decision and the extension did not proceed.

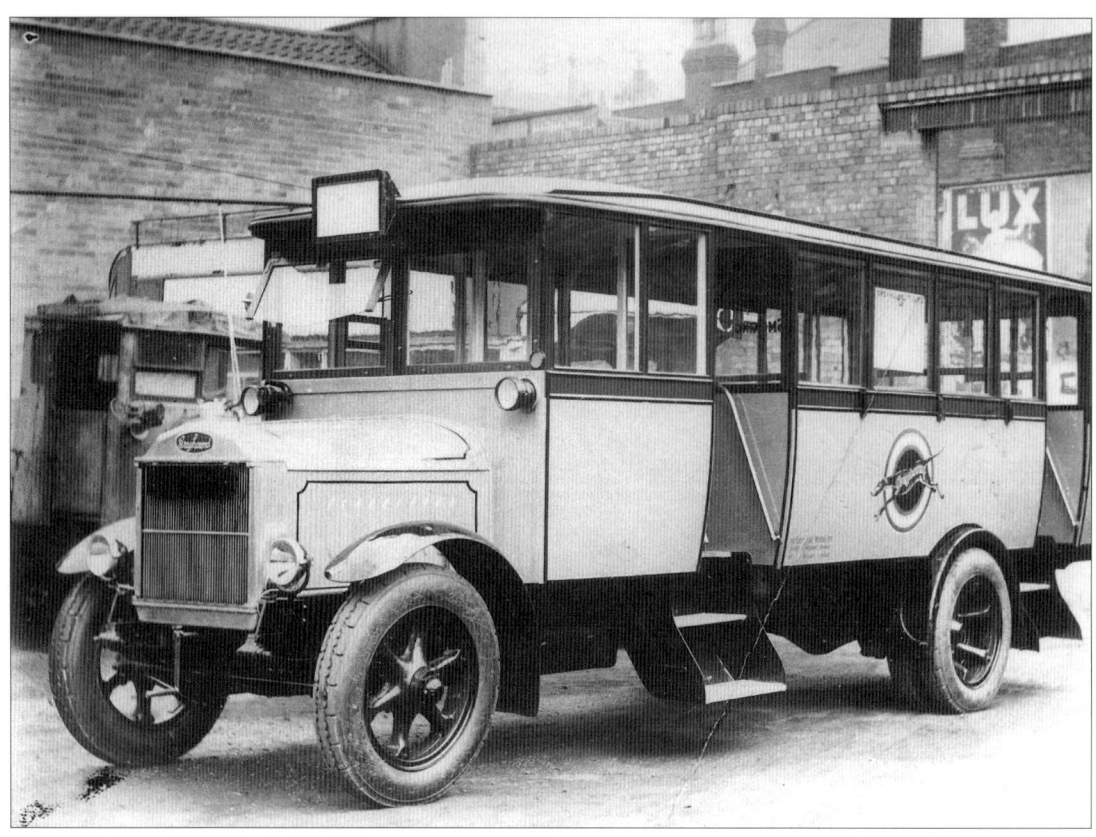

What is believed to be either Y8957 or HR5593, a Dennis 4 tonner acquired in 1926 and fitted with a Strachan and Brown body: note the "Greyhound" on the radiator where the chassis manufacturer's name would normally be.

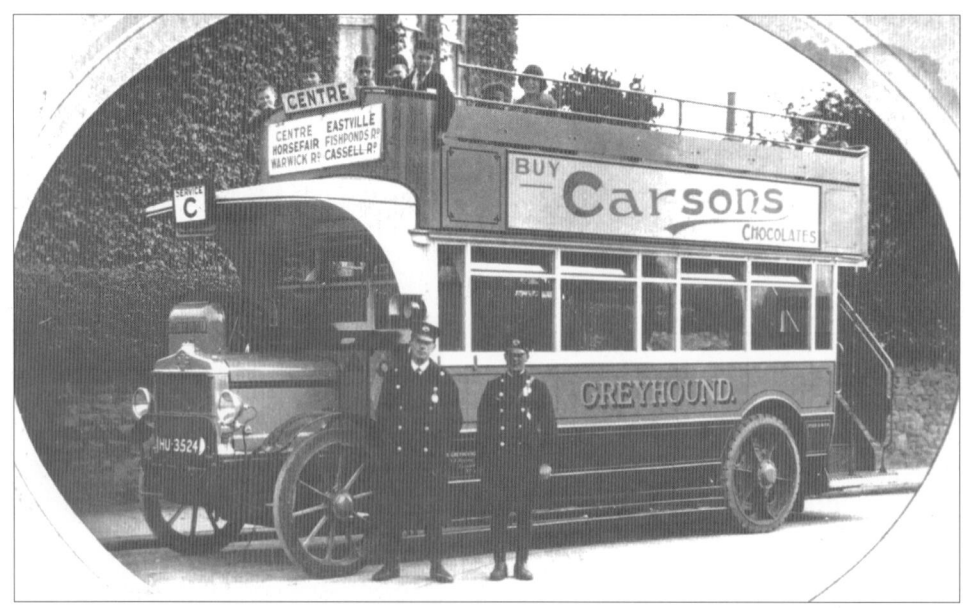

Bristol's first double deckers for almost 20 years were introduced by Greyhound on to their local services in 1926: they were solid tyred open top A.E.C.409 types, like the London General "NS"-types. HU3524 was one of these for use on the Fishponds route, Route C. (Both M.J.Tozer collection).

HU1176, one of the original London coaches seen later in life when running on pneumatic tyres, circa 1928.
(G.Bruce collection).

After the addition of its roof, HU3525 is seen (above) at the Tramways Centre, in company with Bristol Tramways' trams.
(Peter Davey collection).

HU3526 after the fitting of its roof: note that the upper deck window pillars do not line up with those on the lower deck. Also noticeable is that the lower panels have been painted in to the same colour as the main body, instead of the darker colour in which they were delivered. In this view the crew are resplendent in their light coloured dust jackets and white topped hats. (M.J.Tozer collection).

A further view of AEC 409-type HU3526 after fitting of its roof and taken at the Tramways Centre in the company of Bristol Tramway's 4-tonners. (M.Mogridge).

An A.E.C. demonstrator on trade plates 768HX was demonstrated to the Bristol City Council Watch Committee and was fitted with pneumatic tyres, causing them to insist that subsequent double deck buses would no longer be allowed to run on solid tyres. (Commercial Motor).

A general view of Bristol Bridge taken in March 1934 with a closed top A.E.C. 409-type amongst the Bristol Tramways' open topped trams. At the top left is Baldwin Street which leads to the Tramways Centre, whilst the Greyhound A.E.C. is heading in the direction of The Joint Station (later Temple Meads Railway Station.). (G.Bruce collection).

An unusual view of a closed top A.E.C.409, operating along the "Portway", towards Avonmouth, alongside the River Avon at Horshoe Bend. (M.J.Tozer collection).

An unidentified A.D.C. 416-type: note the unusual 38" x 7" tyres mounted on "Simplex" wheels, and the "blacked-out" window over the rear wheel arch which probably hid the stewards' pantry, although these coaches did carry toilets for short while after their introduction. (Bristol Vintage Bus Group collection).

Take Over – Under Bristol Tramways Control, 1928-1935

In February 1928, the following services were listed in the Greyhound timetable:

A. *Sneyd Park – Bedminster Down, daily, via Durdham Downs, Victoria Rooms, Tramways Centre, Joint Station, Bedminster Bridge, Dean Lane, Camden Road, Ashton Avenue, Bedminster Car Terminal, Cross Hands, Bedminster Down (Kings' Head),*

B. *Colston Avenue – Horfield, daily, via top of Stokes Croft, Arches, Fry's Ground, Downend Road, Strathmore Road,*

C. *Colston Avenue – Cassell Road, daily, via Tramways Centre, York Street, St. Nicholas Road, Warwick Road, Marksbury Road, Causeway, Fishponds, Cassell Road,*

D. *Old Market – Ashley Down, daily, via St. Nicholas Road, Sussex Place, Chesterfield Road, Station Road, Ashley Down Road,*

E. *Old Market – Eastville, daily, via Croydon Street, Devon Road, York Road (Bellevue Road), Eastville (tram terminus),*

F. *Bristol – Pill – Portishead, daily, via Prince Street, Ashton tram terminus, Ashton Court Lodges, Beggar Bush Lane, Abbots Leigh (The George), Easton in Gordano, Portbury (The Priory), Sheepway (post box), Albion Hotel, Battery Road, Golf House, Nautical School, Redcliffe Bay,*

G. *Eastville – Horfield – Durdham Downs – Suspension Bridge, daily, via Eastville Robertson Road, Eastville Park, Ashley Hill Station (footpath), Wellington Hotel, Grammar School playing field, Linden Road, Redland Road, Downs (Stoke Road), Zoo,*

H. *Eastville - Fishponds – Kingswood, daily, via Robertson Road, Gloucester Road, Marksbury Road, bottom of Lodge Causeway, Briar Way (Hillfields Avenue), Lodge Hill or Cossham Hospital, Kingswood (Soundwell Road),*

K. *Hotwells- Avonmouth, daily, via Hotwells (tram terminus), Sea Mills Bridge, Sylvan Way, Station Road, Barrow Hill Road, Avonmouth,*

M. *Sherston, Malmesbury, Swindon, daily (including Sundays), via Sherston (High Street), Pinkney (Eagle), Easton Grey (cross roads), The Bull Inn, Malmesbury (Market Place), Black Horse, Lea Turn, Little Somerford Road, Dollars Green Road (post box), Brinkworth (Three Crowns), Suffolk Arms, Callow Hill cross roads, Follywood cross roads, Coped Hall (Prince of Wales), Lydiard cross roads, Wootton Bassett Road, Swindon Town Hall),*

N. *Sherston – Malmesbury – Tetbury – Stroud, Saturday, Sunday and Tuesday only, as above to Malmesbury and then Sunset Hill (Coopers Arms), Long Newnton, Tetbury (Town Hall), Tetbury (Upton), Avening (Bell Inn), Weighbridge Inn, Nailsworth, Inchbrook (Crown Inn), Woodchester (station), Lightpill, Golden Cross, Cainscross, Stroud (King's parade),*

P. *Malmesbury – Sherston –Acton Turville – Bath, Wednesday 2 trips, Monday 1 trip Malmesbury – Sherston, via Malmesbury (the Bull Inn), Easton Grey, Pinkney, Sherston, Luckington, Acton Turville, Toll Down Inn, Sands Hill, Pennsylvania, Nimlet, Bath,*

Q. *Malmesbury – Sherston – Chipping Sodbury – Bristol, Thursday, (also see Malmesbury – Sherston above), – as "P" to Tormarton (Cross Hands), Old Sodbury, Chipping Sodbury, Yate (White Lion), Yate (station), , Nibley, Coalpit Heath (New Inn), Kenlelshire, Downend, Fishponds, Warwick Road, Bristol (Tramways Centre),*

R. *Malmesbury Station – Grittleton – Chippenham, Mondays and Fridays only (3 through trips), as "P to Luckington, then Alderton, Fosse Lodge, Grittleton, Sevington, Bloomfield House, Yatton Keynell, Long Stone Corner, Allington, (Cross roads), Chippenham (Market Place),*

T. *Fishponds (Cassell Road) to Chipping Sodbury, daily, via Downend (Horse Shoe), Kendleshire (Westerleigh Road), Coalpit Heath (Church), Mays Hill (New Inn), Yate (station or White Lion), Chipping Sodbury (clock),*

V. *Knowle – Bushy Park – St. John's Lane – Bedminster Down (Cheddar Grove), daily, via Broad Walk, George Hotel, Bushy Park, Park Avenue, Engineers' Arms, Parson Street,*

Bristol – London, with 41 timing points via Calne and Marlborough, 45 via Devizes.

Then, on March 31st 1928, the Greyhound Company was acquired by Bristol Tramways & Carriage Co. Ltd.

A new company was later formed, called Greyhound Motors (1929) Ltd., as a wholly-owned subsidiary company. Outwardly the public would not have seen any differences as Greyhound's distinctive livery was retained and the name continued to be used to market Greyhound Express services and city services. The Greyhound livery was by this time grey and white with a darkish blue waist rail although one or two vehicles apparently differed slightly. The block lettered "Greyhound" fleetname was being replaced by a bull's-eye motif with a rim of concentric white circles with a red centre on which was superimposed a light grey coloured Greyhound dog at full speed with its front paws lower than its hind quarters. (See photo on rear cover.)

Thought to be Dennis DB1581, this small bus, acquired in 1925, clearly shows the application of the greyhound at speed logo introduced towards the end of the nineteen twenties. (G.Bruce collection).

Greyhound's bus routes and vehicles were numbered into the Bristol Tramways series at this time and the vehicles are listed in Appendix 1. Vehicles of Bristol manufacture were supplied as new equipment from then on.

A further long distance service was started in July 1928 to Weymouth, via Wells, Somerton and Yeovil. Leaving Prince Street at 9:00am and arriving at Weymouth at 1:00pm the return journey left Weymouth at 4:15pm and got to Bristol at 8:15pm. This was supplemented in January 1929 by an alternate route via Whitchurch, Shepton Mallet, Castle Cary, Wincanton and Dorchester taking over from Pioneer.

With the lifting of the 12 mph speed limit for heavy vehicles and the introduction of the new 20 mph limit, Greyhound proposed a number of new routes. These were Coventry to Paignton via Cheltenham, Gloucester, Bath, Bristol and Torquay (once daily each way), London to Bournemouth via Southampton (twice daily) and Bristol to Northampton via Bath, Swindon and Oxford (twice daily), applied for in November 1928 and approved in January 1929 by Bristol Watch Committee.

Typifying the nineteen thirties express scene is HY2703, a Bristol BGW new in May 1931, seen loading with passengers and their luggage at Prince Street, Bristol, whilst operating on the Paignton service. Note the application of a white chassis number just below the waistrail on the bulkhead: this was of course its B.T. & C.C. fleet number as well. The Bristol body type was Q1. (Peter Davey collection)

In addition all of the existing routes were speeded up and an additional London service provided. The total time to London was reduced by 1 hour and 50 minutes. Interavailability of tickets onto Bristol Tramways bus routes was also brought in and passengers could book through for instance from London to Clevedon by using the local bus services from Bristol.

In November 1928 a service commenced between Gloucester and London via Cheltenham and Oxford.

Mr A.E. Bryant (traffic manager) stated, in December 1928, that

> "the London route had run daily since it started in 1925 except for two days early in 1928 when heavy snow made the road impassable. Bad fog at times caused some embarrassment but not beyond cutting off one of the buses."

Local excursions and private hire work was also an important part of the company's activities from the early days and remained so throughout its life. The fleet of Charless Russett (Pioneer) of Days Road, Barton Hill, Bristol was taken over by Bristol Tramways in January 1929 and the entire fleet allocated to Greyhound, with vehicles being kept at Maze Street, Barton Hill Garage, for a short time.

In May 1929 Bournemouth Watch Committee refused an application by Greyhound to increase its licence from 12 to 23 vehicles. This was presumably in connection with the proposed Bournemouth - London service.

Control of the Bristol Tramways & Carriage Co. was assumed by the G.W.R. in 1929 by share purchase but as the G.W.R. did not have powers to operate street tramways the share holding was passed to Western National Omnibus Co. The latter became part of the Tilling Group in February 1931. Any Further route expansion had to be agreed by the railways and other Tilling Group companies. On 10th May 1930, two Liverpool services were started operating jointly with Merseyside Touring Co. of Bootle. One route was via Ross on Wye, Hereford, Ludlow, Shrewsbury and Chester and the other via Cheltenham, Worcester, Wellington, Whitchurch and Warrington: Ribble took over the Merseyside part in 1931. These services were extended south to Torquay in 1931 and in addition Ribble Motor Services applied to operate Preston to Ilfracombe jointly with Greyhound via Warrington and the A49 road.

A Plymouth to Bristol route was started jointly with Royal Blue in April 1930 and Paignton to Bristol via Taunton and Exeter was started on 31st May. A route was started between Birmingham and Torquay via Bromsgrove, Worcester, Tewkesbury, Gloucester, Bristol, Bridgwater, Taunton and Exeter, this route being joint with Midland Red and Royal Blue. 1930 also saw the introduction of a Coventry to Plymouth route via Kenilworth, Stratford-on-Avon, Evesham, Cheltenham, Stroud, Bristol, Taunton and Exeter, taken over from "Pathfinder" of Coventry, and operated jointly with "Royal Blue".

On 16th November 1930 a Bournemouth to London service six times daily was started. This terminated at Clapham Road after calling at 229 Hammersmith Road, Hammersmith. This service was started apparently at the request of the Southern Railway Co. (Presumably for strategic reasons). However after strenuous objections from Royal Blue and others, the application to the Metropolitan traffic commissioners to continue the service in May 1931 was refused on the 22nd of that month and the service had to be curtailed.

A timetable leaflet issued by Greyhound in April 1931 for a service from London to Torquay shows joint participation with Devon General, the G.W.R. and Southern Railway, this route incorporated the London - Bournemouth section refused above. All passengers had to change at Bournemouth as the Bournemouth - Torquay section was worked by Devon General.

Bristol's first modern double decker bus was introduced in 1931. Previously Bristol Tramways had relied on single deckers since 1907 for its needs but now Greyhound was allocated three Bristol G type double deckers, all of which had acted as demonstrators for the Bristol Company's M. C. W. (motor construction works).

Bristol Tramways built several G-type double deck demonstrators in 1931/1932 despite not using double deckers themselves: after demonstration duties throughout the country three of these were allocated to Greyhound services. Greyhound, of course, already used double deckers, albeit of the NS-type. Brush bodied HY3629 is seen here: although the single-deckers and coaches had been receiving black window surrounds since the mid nineteen twenties, the double deck fleet had white window surrounds and roofs. This vehicle was to become the Tramways' C3001.
(Bristol Vintage Bus Group collection).

The 10th March 1932 saw the opening of Victoria Coach Station in London and the

Greyhound London service henceforth started and terminated there.

Also during 1932 negotiations took place concerning the fares on Royal Blue and Greyhound services between London and Weston-Super-Mare the stumbling block being that Greyhound tickets were inter-available on G.W.R. services but as Elliott Brothers, the proprietors of "Royal Blue", were not a railway associated company their fares were not. Royal Blue had been running between Weston and London via Bristol since April 1928.

It was announced in "Motor Transport" on the 7th January 1933 that 'Greyhound Motors Ltd'. Had acquired the whole of the long distance express services of 'Morning Star Motor Services' and had taken over some of their vehicles. The proprietors had gone into voluntary liquidation towards the end of 1932 and a meeting of creditors had been held on 23rd December. The express routes involved were London - Weston-super-Mare via Reading and Bristol, and London - Bristol - Exeter - Torquay and Paignton. Based at 55 Lawrence Hill, Bristol they were to continue their private hire and tours work, it was later announced that as from 1st May 1933 a service would be operated from London to Bristol via Oxford and Swindon from Kings Cross Coach Station at 8:30am daily and return at 3.00 p.m. This was a reinstatement of Morning Star seasonal services.

Four Leyland Lionesses were added to the Greyhound fleet on the takeover of Morning Star Motor Services: United bodied HW659 is seen here at Paddington, near the Charles Rickard's booking office, in Morning Star days.
(G.Bruce collection).

Six new Bristol J type coaches with Bristol bodywork were put into service in May 1933 and were to be Greyhound's last new vehicles.

The final batch of coaches for Greyhound Motor Services included HY9378, a Bristol 26-seat coach bodied Bristol JJW. Its body was of the all metal AM5 type: six similar vehicles were delivered in May 1933.
(Bristol Vintage Bus Group collection).

On 1st July 1934, Greyhound became a founder member of the Associated Motorways pool, based at Cheltenham (which was to become a highly co-ordinated interchange point). All of Greyhound's routes, except the Weston super Mare - Bristol - London service, were vested in the new pool, giving Greyhound a 9.6% share. This share passed to B.T.&.C.C. in January 1936.

1933 coach bodied Bristol JJW, HY9377, is seen in the company of other "Greyhound" coaches in Cheddar George. Note the open roof on a number of the enclosed coaches. The rear of the line includes Bristol Tramways 2 tonners.
(G.Bruce collection).

Seen here when new on Durdham Downs is HY340, a Bristol BGW with Brislington built body new in November 1930 and built to Greyhound's own specification. This was the first Bristol built bus for Greyhound local routes: no doubt the fitting of a roof mounted luggage rack was so that it could be used on express service duplication as required.
(Bristol Vintage Bus Group collection).

The Bristol D-type had the new Bristol six-cylinder JW petrol engine and HY2399 was an early example of the type. The 30-seat bus body again had a roof rack, and additional roof brackets for side mounted destination boards.
(Bristol Vintage Bus Group collection).

HY2399 again, in service outside the Victoria Rooms, Clifton, en route from Clifton to the Tramways Centre. (G.Bruce collection).

HY2701 was the first of the 1931 batch of 6 Bristol B-type coaches, with 26-seat Bristol "Q1" bodies, becoming Bristol Tramways B769 on takeover. (Bristol Tramways).

HY2709, from the same batch, which became Bristol Tramways B764. (Bristol Vintage Bus Group collection).

HY3630 was an ex-Bristol Tramways demonstrator, being a Beadle-bodied Bristol G-type, seating only 44, and being acquired in December 1932. The Tramways had the vehicle back on takeover, when it was renumbered G101. The photograph was taken on the "Portway" and a closed top NS-type is shown travelling in the opposite direction. (M.J.Tozer collection).

Greyhound's only Bristol D-type coach was HY6197 with a 26-seat Bristol "Q2" body, seen here in Marlborough High Street en-route to London from Bristol: the smart driver and conductor with their white topped hats typify the period. The tarpaulin cover on the roof mounted luggage and the side mounted destination boards are also worthy of note. This coach became Tramways' D140. (Bristol Vintage Bus Group collection).

HY6198 was another Bristol G-type former demonstrator to be allocated to Greyhound and is seen en-route to the Tramways Centre: the bus was later to become Tramways' C3002, and with other former Greyhound coaches and buses, was later rebodied. This particular bus received the 1936 Brislington made body from Tramways' 3047, CHY442, in May 1947.
(M.J.Tozer collection).

Official photo of HY9377. (Bristol Tramways).

HY9378, one of six Bristol JJW coaches with Brislington built 26-seat all metal bodies of the AMS type, delivered in 1933 and shown here on a private hire. (Bristol Vintage Bus group collection).

HY9380, a further example of the 1933 Brislington bodied Bristol JJW, becoming J124 on takeover.
(A.G.Vowles).

Only one Albion was ever operated by Greyhound, HW1627, a former "Pioneer" (Russetts) vehicle, here seen at Weymouth on express service. All of Greyhound's express services at this time carried a crew of two, required by the Bristol Watch Committee.
(Bristol Vintage Bus Group collection).

Company demise, 1935, and living on in name only until 1973

On 28th December 1935 an announcement in "Transport World" read as follows:

Greyhound Motors
"Notice to terminate their agreements on 31st December has been received by the employees of the Greyhound Motors Ltd. The Bristol company operate omnibus and long distance coach services. It is understood that the drivers and conductors may not be affected and that The Greyhound Co. will go into voluntary liquidation and be taken over by the B.T & C.C."

This was probably the first that the general public had heard of the impending demise of Greyhound.

Thus on the 1st January 1936 the company was fully absorbed by the Bristol Tramways & Carriage Co. Ltd. Trinity Road coach garage being used by B.T & C.C. as its coach garage for many years and it was later used to store delicenced coaches during the winter and also new vehicles. The garage was sold to the British Railway Board for use as a road vehicle workshop maintenance depot in 1961. The premises are still standing and were being used as a car repair and exhaust centre in 2003 but are now finally empty (2004) awaiting their next fate. A second garage in Maze Street, Barton Hill was apparently retained for several years after transfer from Pioneer in 1929. The offices in Saint Augustin's Parade were absorbed into the B.T & C.C. offices next door but the West Street premises were disposed of in the 1930's.

The Greyhound name was so well known and respected both by the public and the industry that B.T & C.C. retained the name for its tours, excursions and express services involvement and certain front line coaches (See Appendix 4) were fitted with the aluminium stylized Greyhound motifs on each sides.

Under the Tramways' control certain coaches were given the "dog and wheel" motif, the oldest of which was Bristol JJW CHW567. This coach had been on display at the 1935 Olympia show, painted in a gold livery. Used as an ambulance during the war, it was returned to service and lasted as a coach until 1952 and then as a bus until 1958, finally living on as a showman's vehicle until 1967.
(Bristol Vintage Bus Group collection).

Later, in 1960, a new coach livery introduced by Bristol Omnibus Company (as Bristol Tramways & Carriage Company had became in 1958) emphasized this even more by introducing a "Bristol-Greyhound" script fleetname with the greyhound motif placed between the two words, on a cream livery with Crimson trim.

NAE7, 2804, was a 1951 Bristol LL6B full fronted ECW bodied 35-seat coach, and one of the first new coaches after the war to carry the Greyhound logo.
(Bristol Vintage Bus Group collection).

The colours were altered to cream and red in 1963.

The first batch of post war coaches, L6Bs NAE1-3 did not carry the Greyhound logo until they adopted the new red livery. (Bristol Vintage Bus Group collection).

Under the National Bus Company (N.B.C.) administration in 1970, new colours were devised for the coach fleet of the subsidiary companies in the south-west of England. On a base colour of white, each company was to have a distinctive coloured waistband; Bristol Omnibus Company chose magenta and the fleetname BRISTOL GREYHOUND was applied to this waistband in white block capital letters with the white silhouette of a greyhound placed between the two words (a couple of vehicles had these Greyhounds painted in life-like colours.).

This layout was to be short-lived, however as in 1973 the N.B.C. introduced their standard national white livery, with red-and-blue NATIONAL names, throughout the country. The owning company's name appeared just in small letters above the front wheel and on Bristol Omnibus Company coaches this was simplified to the word BRISTOL - the name GREYHOUND had gone, for ever!

HY2713, a former Morning Star Leyland bodied Leyland Tiger that passed to Greyhound with the Morning Star Express services, and subsequently to Bristol Tramways. (J. F. Higham collection).

HY6198, the former Bristol G-type demonstrator, became Tramways' G119 on takeover, then C3002. In 1947 it was fitted with a Gardner oil engine in and a secondhand 56-seat body from 3047. (Bristol Vintage Bus Group collection).

HY3629 was former Bristol G demonstrator G103, the number it retained on transfer, before becoming C3001. It was later fitted with a Gardner oil engine and a lower bonnet line and PV2 radiator together with a new ECW body, seating 59, in July 1950. (Roy Marshall).

Two views of HY9379, former coach bodied Bristol J, J123, renumbered 765 in 1937. It was fitted with a second hand Duple coach body in 1942, and a Gardner oil engine in 1948, then being renumbered 2370. In 1951 the chassis was rehabilitated with lower springs and bonnet line, together with a PV2 radiator and a new Brislington built body to the new post war Tilling standard design. (M.Mogridge).

Bristol J-type HY9382 became J.126 and then 768 on takeover, and later 2373: in July 1941 it received a second hand Brislington built 2-doorway body. It later went on to be rehabilitated and received a new Tilling style body by Longwell Green as seen here in 1946, and was sold to a local showman in 1957. (M.Mogridge).

Duple bodied Bristol L5Gs of the FHT batch carried the Greyhound logo on the side panels: they were ivory and dark blue before the war and green and cream afterwards. (G.Bruce collection).

Duple bodied Bedford WTB FHT817 (fleet number 200) was the only Bedford coach to carry the Greyhound logo: 200 also carried the blue and ivory livery for a short period before the war. (Bristol Vintage Bus Group collection).

The first post war coaches (as opposed to being built with a bus shell body) were NAE1-3, Bristol L6Bs with the new "Queen Mary" style wood framed coach bodies by Eastern Coach Works and seating 31 with a forward entrance door. They were delivered in a Tilling cream with green trim colour scheme, but never carried the Greyhound "dog-in-wheel" logo whilst in this form. They received the logo when they were later repainted into the new colour schemes. NAE2 was 2466.
(Bristol Vintage Bus group collection).

A nearside view of 2466, NAE2, showing the front sliding door, and the additional cab door required to reach the conventional but heavily padded Bristol bonnet cover to check the engine oil level and access the oil filler.
(Bristol Vintage Bus Group collection).

Early in 1961 the three L6B coaches received dark red trim instead of the green they had been delivered with, and were given the aluminium "dog-in-wheel" Greyhound logo. Additionally, the then two survivors had the dark red replaced with bright red in 1963. They were also renumbered into a new coach series starting with 2050, NAE1. (Bristol Vintage Bus Group collection).

A nearside view of 2051, NAE2, as repainted into cream and dark red in the 1961 repainting and renumbering scheme. 2051 did not survive long enough to receive the brighter red colour scheme introduced in 1963. (Bristol Vintage Bus Group collection).

NAE6, 2803, had an 8-feet wide ECW "Queen Mary" style body on its 7 feet 6 inches wide Bristol LL6B chassis: the white steering wheel was to remind the driver of the coach's extra width. The coach is seen outside of the Tramways' office and coach departure point at Prince Street, Bristol. (Bristol Vintage Bus Group collection).

A nearside view of NAE7, 2804, again showing the nearside cab door for accessing the engine: the water filler on the top of the radiator header tank was reached through the lift up flap below the centre of the windscreen, as there was a normal PV2 radiator beneath the full front mouldings. Unlike the NAE1-3 batch, this and subsequent batches carried the "dog-in-wheel" logo from new. (Bristol Vintage Bus Group collection).

Under floor engined coaches joined the Greyhound fleet in 1953 with the Bristol LS: SHT345 is from the second batch delivered a year later, but with Gardner engines rather than the Bristol engines of the first batch. 2094 is seen here with a route board for the Bath City Tour. (Bristol Vintage Bus Group collection).

Two Bristol MW6G coaches joined the Greyhound fleet from South Wales Transport in 1963: they were unique in the Greyhound fleet in having roof quarter lights, ideal for touring. 2135 (279ECY) is seen here in Marlborough whilst operating the London to Bristol and Weston Super Mare service, probably as a duplicate car for the 1967 Bristol RELH coach behind. The date is sometime after 1971, as the following coach carries the recently introduced magenta livery. (M.S.Curtis).

Bristol REs were the mainstay of the Greyhound services during the late nineteen sixties: 2120 (866UAE) is seen here in London's Victoria Coach Station. (A.J.Douglas).

GREYHOUND PHOTOGRAPHS – COLOUR

No colour photographs are known to exist of the original fleet livery: this painting, by Phil Sposito, shows one of the AEC coaches operating in the streets of the capital alongside a London red NS-type double decker. (P. Sposito).

35-seat ECW "Queen Mary" bodied 1951 Bristol LWL6B NHY942, 2810, showing the Tilling Cream and Green livery that was the standard for the "Greyhound" fleet throughout the nineteen fifties. Note the Greyhound "dog-in-wheel" logo, also standard after NAE3. (Bristol Vintage Bus Group collection).

In 1961 2807, NAE10, became 2062 and adopted the new dark red trim colour scheme with the addition of a script fleetname either side of the logo. (G.Bruce).

Although cream and green was the standard colour for the Greyhound coach fleet before the application of red trim in 1961, ECW bodied Bristol LS6B coach 2862, PHW952, was delivered with an experimental trim colour of black, at the time when some fellow Tilling coach fleets were also so painted (such as Crosville and Tilling). No fleet names were carried during this period. (Bristol Vintage Bus Group collection).

Bristol LS6G 2103 (THY955), one of the last batch of 39-seat LS models before the advent of the Bristol MW, seen here in Bath Bus Station in the cream and maroon livery, about to depart on a tour to nearby Longleat. (Bristol Vintage Bus Group collection).

The maroon and cream livery was short lived, and was followed one year later by the maroon being replaced by red, although the script lettering and logo remained. 2111, 404LHT, was a 1961 ECW 39-seat Bristol MW6G. 2111 went on to carry the white and magenta colours. (Bristol Vintage Bus Group collection).

The 20 Bristol RELH6G coaches of 1963/1964, with ECW 45-seat bodies, also carried the distinctive bright cream and red colours throughout the 1960's. One of the batch is seen here entering Bristol Bus and Coach Station en route from London to Weston-super-Mare, on the original express route. (M.Walker).

The last Bristol Greyhound coaches delivered in the red and cream livery were the 1967 batch of E.C.W. bodied Bristol RELH6L vehicles. Three are seen here whilst operating a private hire when new: note the smart drivers in their white topped uniform caps. (Bristol Omnibus).

Another view of one of the 1967 batch of Bristol RELH6L coaches, seen here in Victoria Coach Station, London, early in 1968, loading for the express service to Bristol and Weston Super Mare, having arrived from Southend-on-Sea on hire to Eastern National. (M.Walker).

An official photograph of one of the first Plaxton bodied Leyland Leopard coaches: these coaches were designed for motorway work and introduced the new magenta and white livery to the fleet.
(Bristol Omnibus).

The second batch of Plaxton bodied Leyland Leopards had the Greyhound symbol in accurate colours.
(Bristol Vintage Bus Group collection).

No Bristol Greyhound coaches have been preserved in the short lived cream and maroon livery, although both of the green and cream Bristol L-types shown here would have been eligible for that colour scheme. 1952 Bristol LWL6B 2815(NHY947) is flanked by Bristol L6B 2467 (NAE3) and Bristol MW6G 2138 (BHU92C), all preserved by Mike Walker as part of the Bristol Omnibus Vehicle Collection, and pictured here in May 2009 at the Aust Service Station on the M48 motorway whilst re-enacting the anniversary of the Bristol to North Wales express service. (M.Walker).

Appendix 1: Greyhound Motors Fleet List
Known Vehicles

Fleet No.	Registration	Make	Type	Chassis No.	Body	Seating	Acquired	Disposal	Notes	BTCC number
	AE8311	Dennis	4-ton		Cox&Stephens	Ch29	-/19	10/30	*	
	AE8572	"	"		"	"	-/19	10/30	*	
	AE8839	"	"	12409	"	"	-/19	1/30	*	
1	AE9710	"	"		"	Ch28	-/19	9/33		
3	HT756	"	"		"	"	-/20	10/33		
4	HT1265	"	"	12954	"	"	-/20	1/34		
5	HT1266	"	"		"	"	-/20	9/33		
6	HT1683	"	"		"	Ch29	4/21	7/30		
	HT2542	"			Strachan&Brown	B33F	4/21	10/30		
	HT2625	"	4-ton		"	"	4/21	10/30		
7	HT2626	"	"		Cox&Stephens	Ch27	4/21	7/30	*	
11	HT3518	"	30-cwt		"	Ch15	5/21	9/28		
2	HT3519	"	4-ton		"	Ch23	5/21	6/31		
9	HT3520	"	3-ton	20010	"	Ch27	5/21	9/33		
10	HT3521	"	"		"	"	5/21	9/33		
8	HT3522	"	"		"	"	5/21	/24		
12	HT3525	"	"		"	Ch28	5/21	9/33		
14	HT3535	"	"		"	"	5/21	12/32		
	HT4327	Crossley				Ch7	5/21	10/25		
	HT4499	Dennis	4-ton	40011	Strachan&Brown	B32F	11/21	12/35		
	HT4501	"	"	40017	"	B32F	11/21	12/35		
15	XB8140	"	WOS			Ch29	By/21	2/27	(a)	
	HT4592	"	4-ton	40031	Strachan&Brown	B26D	1/22	1/34	(t)	
	HT4593	"	"		"	B32F	1/22	-/34		
	HT4818	"	"		"	B34R	4/22	-/32		
	HT4819	A.E.C.	YC	13710	Hora	B32RP	5/22	11/25	(b)	
	HT4820	"	"	13702	"	"	6/22	11/26	(b)	
	HT5322	Dennis	4-ton		Strachan&Brown	B32F	6/22	-/30		
	HT5324	"	"		"	"	6/22	-/32		
	HT4808	A.E.C.	YC	13706	Hora	B32RP	8/22	3/26	(b)	
	AE8023	Daimler	CB		Strachan&Brown	B25R	-/23	-/30	(c)	
	HT8768	Dennis	4-ton		"	B30F	9/23	-/30		

Fleet No.	Registration	Make	Type	Chassis No.	Body	Seating	Acquired	Disposal	Notes	BTCC number
	HT8769	"	"		"	"	9/23	-/30		
19	HU28	"	"	40362	Cox&Stephens	C27D	6/24	7/31		
17	HU879	"	"		"	C32F	6/24	7/31		
8	T7174	"	3-ton	12621	TorquayCarriageCo	Ch28	6/24	8/31	(d)	
	BL9469	"	4-ton	10510	Strachan&Brown	B32F	8/24	12/30	(c)	
	HU991	"	"		"	B30F	10/24	-/30		
18	AF2221	"	"			Ch30	4/25	-/31	(g)	
	DB1581	"	30-cwt		Dennis	B18F	-/25	10/27	(f)	
16	DB1828	"			"	Ch?	-/25	-/31	(f)	
	HU1176	"	4-ton		Strachan&Brown	C23F	3/25	7/32	(x)	
	HU1177	"	"		"	"	3/25	7/32	(x)	
	HU3523	"	"		"	B26R	8/25	1/34		
	HU3524	A.E.C.	409	409018	Short Bros.	O28/24ROS	10/25	1/36		A11
	HU3525	"	"	409022	"	"	1/26	1/36		A12
	HU3526	"	"	409018	"	"	1/26	1/36		A13
	HU4316	Dennis			Strachan&Brown	B23D	12/25	2/35		
	HU4804	A.E.C.	411	411122	"	FC26F	3/26	1/36		A14
	HU4805	"	"	411123	"	"	3/26	1/36		A15
	HU4808	"	"	411160	"	"	3/26	1/36		A16
	HU4809	"	"	411161	"	"	3/26	1/34		
	HU5145	Dennis	G		"	C32F	4/26	1/30		
	HU5150	A.E.C.	409	409032	Short Bros.	H28/24ROS	4/26	1/36		A17
	HU5152	Dennis	G		Strachan&Brown	C32F	4/26	1/30		
	Y8957	"	4-ton	9538	"	B32D	4/26	7/30	(u)	
	HU6625	"	G	50838	"	B24D	7/26	1/34		
	HU6626	"	2 1/2ton	45411	"	B26F	7/26	7/32	(h)	X176
	HU7240	A.E.C.	409	409090	Short Bros.	H28/24ROS	11/26	1/36	(k)	A18
	HR5593	Dennis	4-ton	40010	Strachan&Brown	C32	12/26	12/27	(j)	
	HU8157	A.E.C.	NS		Short Bros.	H28/24ROS	4/27	9/27	(l)	
	HU8158	"	"		"	"	4/27	9/27	(l)	
	HU8159	"	"		"	"	4/27	9/27	(l)	
	HU8161	Dennis	G		Strachan&Brown	B26F	4/27	1/36		
	HU9634	A.D.C.	416A	416009	"	C32F	6/27	1/36		A100
	HU9635	"	"	416183	"	"	6/27	1/36		A101

Fleet No.	Registration	Make	Type	Chassis No.	Body	Seating	Acquired	Disposal	Notes	BTCC number
	HU9637	"	"	416006	"	C28F	7/27	1/36		A103
	HU9638	"	"	416008	"	"	7/27	1/36		A104
	HU9639	"	"	416007	"	"	7/27	1/36		A105
	HU9640	"	"	416005	"	"	7/27	1/36		A106
	XW9868	A.E.C.	413	413001	"	C28F	7/27	1/36	(m)	A10
	IA4322	"				B32F	8/27	?	(n)	
	HR2646	Dennis	4-ton	12855	Bartle	"	9/27	-/29	(o)	
	HR2647	"	"	12823	Bartle	"	9/27	-/29	(o)	
	HW1626	"			Strachan&Brown	B32R	4/28	10/30		
	HW3642	Bristol	B	B335	Bristol N	C24F	12/28	1/36		B335
	HW3643	"	"	B339	"	"	12/28	1/36		B339
	HW3644	"	"	B343	"	"	12/28	1/36	(v)	B343
	HW3645	"	"	B342	"	"	12/28	1/36	(v)	B342
	HW3646	"	"	B337	"	"	1/29	1/36		B337
	HW3647	"	"	B334	"	"	1/29	1/36		B334
	HW3648	"	"	B336	"	"	2/29	1/36	(v)	B336
	HW3649	"	"	B340	"	"	2/29	1/36		B340
	HW3650	"	"	B341	"	"	2/29	1/36	(v)	B341
	HT3729	Daimler				Ch	1/29	4/39	(p)	
	HU4806	A.E.C/	507	507006	Strachan&Brown	B32F	1/29	1/36	(p)	Bence
	HU5143	Reo			"	C20F	1/29	/32	(p)	
	HU7234	A.E.C.	507	507072	"	C32F	1/29	1/36	(p)	A21
	HU8169	"	"	507076	"	"	1/29	1/36	(p)	A109
	HU9636	A.D.C.	416A	416152	"	FB32F	1/29	1/36	(p)	A102
	KB1999	A.E.C.	YC		?	B?R	1/29	1/30	(p)	
	HW1627	Albion	PM26	7023C	Russett	B32F	1/29	1/36	(p)(w)	A3
	HW2551	A.D.C.	416A	416824	Strachan&Brown	C32F	1/29	1/36	(p)	A107
15	HW2553	Reo			?		1/29	1/30	(p)	
	HW3105	A.D.C.	416A	416645	Strachan&Brown	C32F	1/29	1/30	(p)	A108
	HW9052	Bristol	B	B657	Northern Counties	C26F	5/30	1/36		B657
	HW9053	"	"	B658	"	"	5/30	1/36		B658
	HW9054	"	"	B659	"	"	5/30	1/36		B659
	HW9055	"	"	B661	"	"	5/30	1/36		B661
	HW9056	"	"	B660	"	"	5/30	1/36		B660

Fleet No.	Registration	Make	Type	Chassis No.	Body	Seating	Acquired	Disposal	Notes	BTCC number
	HW9057	"	"	B663	"	"	5/30	1/36	(v)	B663
	HW9506	"	"	B662	"	"	6/30	1/36		B662
	HW9507	"	"	B664	"	"	6/30	1/36		B664
	HW9508	"	"	B668	"	"	6/30	1/36		B668
	HW9509	"	"	B665	"	"	6/30	1/36		B665
	HW9510	"	"	B666	"	"	6/30	1/36		B666
	HW9571	"	"	B664	"	"	6/30	1/36		B664
	HY340	"	"	B703	Bristol L10	B31D	11/30	1/36		B703
	HY731	"	"	B652	"	"	11/30	1/36		B652
	HY732	"	"	B654	"	"	11/30	1/36		B654
	HY733	"	"	B655	"	"	11/30	1/36		B655
	DF6308	A.E.C.	426	426197	Bence	C32F	11/30	1/36	(q)	A19
	HY2399	Bristol	D	D115	Bristol L6.2	B30F	5/31	1/36		D115
	HY2701	"	B	B769	" Q1	C26F	5/31	1/36		B769
	HY2702	"	B	B770	"	"	5/31	1/36		B770
	HY2703	"	B	B766	"	"	5/31	1/36		B766
	HY2704	"	B	B768	"	"	5/31	1/36		B768
	HY2708	"	B	B767	"	"	6/31	1/36		B767
	HY2709	"	B	B764	"	"	6/31	1/36		B764
	HY3629	"	G	G103	Brush	H24/24R	12/32	1/36	(r)	G103
	HY3630	"	"	G101	Bristol	H24/20R	12/32	1/36	(r)	G106
	HY6197	"	D	D140	" Q2	C26F	6/32	1/36		D140
	HY6198	"	G	G119	Beadle 269	H26/26R	12/32	1/36	(r)	G119
	HW658	Leyland	PLC1	45902	United	C26F	1/33	1/36	(s)	L1
	HW1635	"	"	47179	"	"	1/33	1/36	(s)	L2
	HW3102	"	"	47475	R.Davis, Bristol	"	1/33	1/36	(s)	L3
	HW3103	"	"	47476	"	"	1/33	1/36	(s)	L4
	HW9588	"	TS3	61227	Leyland	DP32F	1/33	1/36	(s)	L700
	HY1	"	"	61226	"	"	1/33	1/36	(s)	L701
	HY2713	"	"	61746	"	"	1/33	1/36	(s)	L702
	HY2716	"	"	61747	"	"	1/33	1/36	(s)	L703
	HY9377	Bristol	J	J110	Bristol AM5	C26F	5/33	1/36		J110
	HY9378	"	"	J111	"	"	5/33	1/36		J111
	HY9379	"	"	J123	"	"	5/33	1/36		J123
	HY9380	"	"	J124	"	"	5/33	1/36		J124
	HY9381	"	"	J125	"	"	5/33	1/36		J125
	HY9382	"	"	J126	"	"	5/33	1/36		J126

NOTES:-

Fleet numbers were allocated only to charabancs, the buses were identified by the local hackney carriage numbers, which were displayed on the front bulkhead inside the saloon in white figures. Fleet numbers were first introduced around 1920, being discontinued about 1934.

The chassis of the first nineteen vehicles listed were all new as War Office lorries dating from the 1916 to 1918 period, and were acquired from the War Office Disposal Board. It is believed that most, if not all, were used as lorries by Greyhound when first acquired, receiving passenger bodies between 1919 and 1921.

- * These vehicles were rebodied by Strachan & Brown as buses by 1924: most were B33D
- a XB 8140 was acquired as a lorry, being rebodied as a charabanc in 1921
- b HT 4591/4808/19/20 came from Liverpool Corporation Tramways and were new in 1919 as KB 1999, K1972, K 1971, K1978 respectively. Note that a mystery vehicle was acquired from "Pioneer"(C.Russett) in 1929 also registered KB 1999.
- c AE 8023 came from an unknown owner, being bodied as a bus in 1923.
- d T 7174 was purchased from the South Devon Garages Ltd., Torquay ,(Grey Cars) and was new in 1919.
- e BL 9469 was new to Shepardson, Wokingham, Berks as a lorry in 1922.
- f DB 1581, DB 1828 were first registered by Dennis Brothers Ltd. of Guildford as new vehicles.
- g AF 2221 was purchased from Smiths Motors (Cornwall) Ltd, Falmouth, and new in 1919.
- h To BT&CC 10/36 XI76.
- j HR 5593 came from Shrewton Motor Services (Hall), Orcheston, Wilts. New 1921.
- k HU 5150 was Greyhound's first AEC 409 to be fitted with pneumatic tyres from new.
- l HU 8157-9 had only a short life with Greyhound. They were standard L.G.O.C. NS types and carried L.G.O.C. bonnet numbers NS 2051-3. They were returned to AEC Ltd. (dealer) in 1927.
- m XW 9868 was purchased from AEC Ltd. (dealer). It had been first licensed to L.G.O.C. as their fleet No. Rl with chassis number 2308. New 1925, it was rebuilt by A.E.C. to a 413-type in 1927.
- n IA 4322 was acquired as a lorry 08/27 from an unknown owner.
- o HR 2646/7 came from Anna Valley Motor Services, Tisbury, Wilts in 1927. They had been new in 1919 as lorries and received bus bodies in 1924.
- p These vehicles were acquired from C.F. Russett, Bristol (Pioneer) in January 1929. The origin of KB 1999 is not known as the original vehicle with this registration was re-registered by Greyhound in 1922.
- q DF6308 came from Bence, Hanham, and was new in 1928.
- r HY 3629/30, HY 6198 were formerly Bristol Tramways & Carriage Co. Ltd. demonstrators.
- s These vehicles were acquired from E.C. Jones & Sons Ltd., Bristol (Morning Star Motor Services). They were new in 1928 (the HW's and HU9588), 1930 (HY1/2713) and 1931 (HY 2716).

- t HT 4592 was later B32.
- u Y8957 came from Montgomery, Bridgwater, as a lorry. Rebodied 1926.
- v HW3644-6/8/50 and HW9057 at least were later relegated to bus duties..
- w HU1627 is recorded in Albion records as being a Russett body, but it is thought that this was bodied by either Strachans & Brown, R.Davis of Horfield or Morrish, Bristol.
- x Built as 24-seaters, the rear seat obscuring the emergency exit was removed when new.

Deliveries from 1926 had pneumatic tyres and by 1928 existing solid tyred vehicles had been converted to pneumatics, except for the three open-top NS types which were not so fitted until 1931 when they had their top deck covers fitted.

From Bristol Hackney records we can record some of the routes to which certain vehicles were allocated.

Location	Vehicles
Avonmouth	HU5145, HU5150, HU5152, HU8157, HU8158, HU8159
Ashley Down	AE8311, HT2542, HT2625, HT4592, HT5322, HT8769
Ashley Down/Eastville	HT5324
Kingswood/Fishponds	HR2646, HR2647
Sneyd Park	HT4499, HT4818, HU3523, HU4316, HU8161
Portishead	AE8572, AE8839
Dundry	HT4501, HT8768, BL9469
Chipping Sodbury	DB1581
Malmesbury	IA4322, HR5593

Known Service Vehicles

Reg.No	Manufacturer	Body Type	Date Acquired	Date withdrawn
AE9431	Berna	Lorry	1919	1928
AR6309	Dennis	"	?	1930
K1776	Thornycroft	"	?	1927
K1778	"	"	?	1927
XL554	Ford T	Breakdown	1922	1935
DR7440	Morris Cowley	Van	1925	1935
NH4986	Dennis	Petrol tanker	?	?
HW3211	Austin A6	Staff car	1928	1935
HY9580	Austin A6	Staff car	1930 new	1935

Taxi Fleet

Reg.No	Manufacturer	Body Type	Date Acquired	Date withdrawn
AE4506	Charron	Taxi	1920 new	1926
AE4507	"	"	"	"
AE4508	"	"	"	"

Appendix 2: Charles Russett Fleet List

Known Vehicles

Charles Russett (general haulier) 1897 Stanley Mews, Stanley Hill, Totterdown
C. F. Russett (brake proprieter) by 1910 22, Queen Ann Road and Maze Street, Barton Hill
C. H. Russett, "Pioneer" 45 Days Road, Barton Hill

Registration	Make	Type	Chassis No.	Body	Seating	Acquired	Sold	Disposal
?	Maudsley	22HP			Ch28	5/14	?	?
AE4194	Clement Talbot				Ch22	5/14	1/29	Bristol Tramways (not used)
AE6639	Pierce Arrow	3 ton			Ch	-/16	by 1/29	C.Russett, Bristol, lorry
AE8816	Commer				Ch	-/18	by 1/26	"
AE9391	Pierce Arrow				Ch23	-/19	by 1/23	"
AE9739	Clement Talbot				Ch14	1/20	10/21	H.Russett, Combe Martin
OB2028	Pierce Arrow				Ch23	by -/20	?	"
HT779	Clement Talbot				Ch14	3/20	1/29	?, Berkshire
HT937	Karrier			lorry/chara		3/20	?	C.Russett, Bristol, lorry
HT1765	"			"		3/20	7/28	Bristol Tramways (not used)
HT1945	"			"		4/20	1/29	"
HT2149	"			"		4/20	1/29	Alcock, Weston-S-Mare
HT2994	Karrier				Ch	3/21	by 7/26	C.Russett , Bristol, lorry
HT3070	Dennis	3 ton		Morrish	B30F	4/21	5/26	Wincanton Transport ,lorry
HT3517	"	"			Ch27	6/21	5/26	?
HT3616	Buick				Ch7	7/21	by 5/30	Hodges, Combe Martin
HT3729	Daimler				Ch23	7/21	by 5/30	C Russett, Bristol, lorry
HT4357	"				Ch26	11/21	7/27	Scrapped
HT4358	Dennis	3 ton		Morrish	B30F	11/21	7/28	Bristol Tramways (not used)
HT4361	Daimler				Ch26	11/21	by 1/29	"
HT4591	A.E.C.	YC	13290	Hora	B32RP	4/22	6/28	Not traced
KB1999	"	"			B—R	by -/22	1/29	Greyhound, Bristol
HT5743	Daimler				Ch	7/22	by 1/29	C.Russett, Bristol, lorry
T6970	A.E.C.	YC	14228		Ch	10/22	4/26	Bristol Tramways (not used)
HT6357	Buick				Ch6	12/22	?	Not traced
PC9201	Dennis				B27	5/23	7/26	F.Martin, Cheltenham
NK1548					B	by 1/24	?	?
CW4075	F.I.A.T.		880580		Ch14	8/24	11/24	Bath Tramways Motor Co.
HU4806	A.E.C.	507	507006	Strachan&Brown	?	1/26	1/29	Greyhound, Bristol
HU5143	Reo			"	C20F	4/26	1/29	"
HU5147	A.E.C.			"	C32F	4/26	1/29	"
LX9063	"	Y			B--F	7/26	9/26	F.Martin, Cheltenham
HU7234	"	507	507072	Strachan&Brown	C32F	9/26	1/29	Greyhound, Bristol
HU8169	"	"	507076	"	"	6/27	1/29	"
HU9636	ADC	416A	416152	"	FB32F	?	1/29	"
HW1627	Albion	PMA28	7023C	Russett	B32F	4/28	1/29	"
HW2551	ADC	416A	416824	Strachan&Brown	C32F	5/28	1/29	"
HW2553	Reo			"	C20F	5/28	1/29	"
HW3105	ADC	416A	416645	"	C32F	10/28	1/29	"

NOTES:-

AE6639	was named "Pioneer No.1".
HT937	was "Pioneer No.3".
HT3070	also had a charabanc body at some time.
HT4591	was acquired from Liverpool City Tramways and was new in 1919. It was re-registered when acquired, having been KB1999 originally.
KB1999	is a mystery vehicle as both HT4591 and KB1999 are recorded as current at the same time in Bristol hackney records.
T6970	came from Hollis & Shapcott, Combe Martin, as a charabanc. It was new in 6/19.
PC9201	is believed to have been first registered by Dennis Brothers, Guildford.
NK1548	has not been identified further.
CW4075	came from Manning, Birkdale, and was new in 1/22.
LX9063	is believed to have been a lorry when acquired.
HW1627	the body recorded by Albion as by Russett, but may have been by Strachan & Brown, Morrish or Davis.

The following former buses or charabancs were purchased for use as lorries, although their use for carrying passengers cannot be ruled out:

Reg.No.	Manufacture	Type	Former owner	Date acquired
HT9740	A.E.C.	Y	Wm.Russett, Bristol	?
DY2404	Leyland		Skinner, Hastings	?
EL1889	"			?
L9267	Napier		Feltham, Kingswood	7/27
AE9468	Thornycroft			-/20
FX4431	A.E.C.	3 ton	Tutt, Gosport	by 12/27
HT2110	Bristol	4 ton	Western Roadways, Bristol	8/30
HT2645	"	"	"	8/30
Y5432	Dennis	4 ton	Premier, St.Phillips	c32

Appendix 3: Morning Star Fleet List

Known Vehicles, 1916 to 1/1933

E. Jones, Morning Star, 55, Lawrence Hill, Bristol

30, Easton Road, Bristol

Fleet No.	Reg.no.	Make	Type	Chassis No.	Body	Seating	Acquired	Sold	Disposal
1	AE6543	Leyland				Ch32	-/16	by 1/30	E.Jones, lorry
	AE8797	Crossley	26hp			Ch7	-/19	10/30	?
11	HT162	"	X			Ch14	1/21	11/31	E.Cox, Frome
14	HT6316	Leyland		10001	Leyland	Ch14	10/22	by 9/41	?
4	HT6510	"	G7		"	Ch33	1/23	by 9/35	E.Jones, lorry
6	XE3455	"	RAF			Ch27	by 7/24	by 12/30	"
	NK7554	"	"			Ch	by 7/24	by 12/27	"
5	EL1889	"				Ch28	by 7/24	by 12/27	C Russett, Bristol, lorry
7	HU878	"	RAF	23264	Leyland	Ch	7/24	12/27	?
8	BL1929	Crossley		10431		Ch14	6//25	6/28	?
9	FR4399	Leyland	M	12215	Leyland	Ch27	6/25	by 12/30	E.Jones, lorry
15	MR1642	Lancia	Z	4288		Ch26	by 6/25	12/26	"
10	HU3990	Crossley				Ch14	7/25	4/28	Hancock, Hewish
3	XE1727	Napier				Ch14	by 7/25	by 12/30	?
	CX2542	Leyland				Ch	9/26	9/28	E.Jones, lorry
15	LX8984	"	S5	10216		Ch32	12/26	3/37	?
	HW658	"	PLC1	45902	United	C26F	2/28	1/33	Greyhound
	HW1635	"	"	47197	"	"	5/28	1/33	"
	HW2558	Bean				C14	6/28	9/35	Scrapped
	HW3102	Leyland	PLC1	47475	R.Davis	C26F	6/28	1/33	Greyhound
	HW3103	"	"	47476	"	"	8/28	1/33	"
12	MR1156	"	M	10900	Leyland	Ch28	5/29	by 12/30	?
	HW5648	"	LTB1	50266	"	C26F	7/29	8/37	
	HW5649	"	"	50280	"	"	7/29	8/37	
	HW9062	Sunbeam	Panther	K11123	Short	C26D	5/30	2/42	Bengry, Leominster
	HR8821	Leyland	G7	12116		C32	6/30	8/33	
	HW9588	"	TS3	61227	Leyland	DP32F	7/30	1/33	Greyhound
	HY1	"	TS3	61226	"	"	7/30	1/33	"
	HY748	"	KP1	5	"	C20F	7/30	9/39	War department
	HY2713	"	TS3	61746	"	DP32F	7/31	1/33	Greyhound
	HY2716	"	"	61747	"	"	7/31	1/33	"

PREVIOUS OWNERS

XE3455, NK7554, EL1899, BL1929, CX2542, XE1727	Not known
FR4349	?, London
MR1642	F.Barnes, Trowbridge
LX8984	Cambrian, Landray, London
MR1156	Goulding, Trowbridge
HR8821	Christy & Long, Bristol

NOTE:-

Morning Star operated a large fleet of lorries which were numbered in the same series as the P.S.V. fleet.

Appendix 4

Bristol Tramways & Bristol Omnibus Company vehicles, which carried the Greyhound motif or "Bristol Greyhound", fleet names.

'A'	Greyhound motif				On Ivory/Dark Blue			
'AA'					On Cream/Tilling Green			
2144 - 2156	FHT 781 -793	Bristol	L5G	Duple	C32F	1939 to 1952	A. AA
200	FHT 817	Bedford	WTB	Duple	C20F	1939 to 1947	A. AA
2367	CHW 567	Bristol	J(5G)	BBW	C26F	1946 to 1951	AA
2801 - 2807	NAE 4 – 10	Bristol	LL6B	E.C.W.	FC35F	1951 to 1961	AA
2808 - 2817	NHY 940 – 949	Bristol	LWL6B	E.C.W.	FC35F	1951 to 1961	AA
2818 - 2827	OHY 990 – 999	Bristol	LWL6B	E.C.W.	FC37F	1952 to 1961	AA
2858 - 2867	PHW 948 – 957	Bristol	LS6B	E.C.W.	C39F	1953 to 1961	AA *
2868 - 2877	SHT 341 – 350	Bristol	LS6G	E.C.W.	C39F	1954 to 1961	AA *
2878 - 2882	THY 952 – 956	Bristol	LS6G	E.C.W.	C39F	1955 to 1961	AA
2934 - 2988	289 – 293 HHU	Bristol	MW6G	E.C.W.	C39F	1960 to 1961	AA

* some of these were initially cream/black or cream/maroon

'B'	Bristol Greyhound				Maroon/Cream Livery	
2050 – 2052	NAE 1 – 3	Bristol	L6B	E.C.W.	FC31F	1961 – 1962 (2051) 1961 – 1963 (2050/3)
2053 – 2059	NAE 4 – 10	Bristol	LL6B	E.C.W.	FC35F	1961 – 1962
2060 – 2069	NHY 940 – 949	Bristol	LWL6B	E.C.W.	FC35F	1961 – 1963/4
2070 – 2079	OHY 990 – 999	Bristol	LWL6B	E.C.W.	FC37F	1961 - 1964
2080 – 2089	PHW 948 – 957	Bristol	LS6B	E.C.W.	C39F	1961 - 1964
2090 – 2099	SHT 341 – 950	Bristol	LS6G	E.C.W.	C39F	1961 - 1964
2100 – 2104	THY 952 – 956	Bristol	LS6G	E.C.W.	C39F	1961 - 1964
2105 – 2109	289 – 293 HHU	Bristol	MW6G	E.C.W.	C39F	1961 - 1964
2110 – 2114	403 – 407 LHT	Bristol	MW6G	E.C.W.	C39F	1961 - 1964

'C'	Bristol Greyhound				Bright Red/Cream Livery	
2050/2052	NAE 1/3	Bristol	L6B	E.C.W.	FC31F	1963 – 1964
2060 – 2069	NHY 940 – 949	Bristol	LWL6B	E.C.W.	FC35F	1963/4 – 1964/5
2070 – 2079	OHY 990 – 999	Bristol	LWL6B	E.C.W.	FC37F	1964 - 1964
2080 – 2089	PHW 948 – 957	Bristol	LS6B	E.C.W.	C39F	1964 – 1965
2090 – 2099	SHT 341 – 950	Bristol	LS6G	E.C.W.	C39F	1964 - 1965
2100 – 2104	THY 952 – 956	Bristol	LS6G	E.C.W.	C39F	1964 – 1967
2105 – 2109	289 – 293 HHU	Bristol	MW6G	E.C.W.	C39F	1964 - 1971
2110 – 2114	403 – 407 LHT	Bristol	MW6G	E.C.W.	C39F	1964 – 1973 except 2112
2115 – 2124	861 – 870 UAE	Bristol	RELH6G	E.C.W.	C45F	1963 – 1971/2
2125 – 2134	971 980 WAE	Bristol	RELH6G	E.C.W.	C45F	1964 – 1973/4
2135/2136	279/280 ECY	Bristol	MW6G	E.C.W.	C39F	1963 – 1971
2137 –2143	BHU 91 –97 C	Bristol	MW6G	E.C.W.	DP39F	1965 – 1971
2144 – 2150	FHW 150 – 156 D	Bristol	MW6G	E.C.W.	C39F	1966 – 1971
2151 – 2156	NHW 308 –315 F	Bristol	RELH6L	E.C.W.	DP45F	1968 – 1970-72

'D'	"Bristol Greyhound" fleetnames				White and Magenta Livery	
2105 – 2109	289 – 295 HHU	Bristol	MW6G	E.C.W.	C39F	1971 to 1973
2110 – 1/3 – 4	403/4/6/7 LHT	Bristol	MW6G	E.C.W.	C39F	1971 to 1973
2115 – 2124	861 – 870 UAE	Bristol	RELH6B	E.C.W.	C47F	1971/2 to 1973/4
2125 – 2134	971 – 980 WAE	Bristol	RELH6B	E.C.W.	C47F	1971 to 1972 – 4
2135 – 2136	279/280 ECY	Bristol	MW6G	E.C.W.	C39F	1971 to 1973
2144 – 2150	FHW 150 – 156 D	Bristol	MW6G	E.C.W.	C39F	1971 to 1973
2151 –2156	NHW 308 – 313F	Bristol	RELH6L	E.C.W.	DP45F	1970 – 2 to 1973
2157/8	YHU 521/522 J	Leyland	PSU3A/4R	Plaxton	C47F	1971 to 1972
2159/2160	BHW 84/85 J	Leyland	PSU3B/4R	Plaxton	C47F	1971 to 1973
301	UFJ 230 J	Bristol	RELH6L	Plaxton	C49F	1972 to 1972
308	UUO 453 J	Bristol	RELH6L	Plaxton	C44F	1972 to 1972
407	YTX 323 H	Leyland	PSU3A/4R	Plaxton	C47F	1972 to 1972
2161 - 2163	EHW 313 –315K	Bristol	RELH6G	Plaxton	C47F	1972 to 1973/4

Notes

301/8, 407 were on loan from Greenslades

NAE3, NHY 947, 404/5/6 LHT, BHU 92C, FHW 154/6D, are in preservation, 404/5/6 LHT as towing vehicles.

Appendix 5

The bus services transferred to Bristol Tramways in 1936

WTA Ref No.	Service	Route	Average Frequency	B.T.&C.C. Route
H28	A	Now diverted via Coronation Rd, Beauley Rd, Raleigh Rd, Duckmoor Rd, Luckwell Rd, and Winterstoke Rd, Bedminster Down Rd to Brunel Rd.	30 mins	22
H27	B	Now extended via Milner Rd, Purdown rd to Horfield Barracks. A further extension applied for in March 1931 to Temple Meads Station Yard from the Centre via Baldwin St & Victoria St was refused.	10/20 mins	21A
H32	C	Extended in 1935 to Downend (Horse Shoe Inn) via Overnhill Rd and Downend Rd, returning via Badminton Rd, Cleeve Rd and Bromley Heath Rd.	15/20 mins	84
H29	D	Old Market (Careys Lane) to Horfield (Filton Avenue, Eden Grove) via Old Market St, Lawford St, St.Mathias Park, Stratton St, Newfoundland St, Newfoundland Rd, Grosvenor Rd, Sussex Place, Ashley Hill, Ashley Down Rd, Milner Rd, Purdown Rd, Muller Rd, Filton Avenue. (Also noted via St.Nicholas Rd & Chesterfield Rd). Applied to extend beyond Eden Grove as soon as northern end of Filton Avenue is dedicated as a public highway and to extend from Old Market St to Temple Meads via (a) Tower Hill, Temple Way or (b) via Midland Rd and Broad Plain.	10 mins	81
	E	Old Market to Kingswood (Soundwell Rd)		Ceased
H35	F	Bristol to Portishead (Redcliffe Bay)	20/30 mins	85
H31	G	Eastville (Robertson Rd) to Clifton Suspension Bridge via Horfield and Redland. Extended in 1934 to Old Market and re-routed between Old Market (Careys Lane) and Eastville to run via Easton Rd, Devon Rd and Robertson Rd.	30 mins	83
H31	H	Old Market – Whitehall – Fishponds – Kingswood.		Ceased
H33 H34	K	Extended to Prince St. this had been a joint service. By 1931, Tramway Centre to Clifton Zoo via College Green, Park St, Queens Rd, Pembroke Rd, Upper Belgrave Rd and Durdham Downs	5/20 mins Saturdays to Wednesdays inclusive during Easter, Whitson and August Bank Holidays.	99

NOTES

Further services transferred to B.T.& C.C. were:-
Good Friday and Sundays only outwards to Hotwells only to meet P & A Campbell's steamers at Hotwells Landing stage from Eastville Park, Avonmouth (Gloucester Row), Staple Hill (High Street / Victoria Street), Horfield (Filton Avenue / Muller Road), Hillfields (Thicket Avenue / Briar Way), Netham / Marsh Lane Bridge / Feeder Road. When the passengers got home in the evening they had to use the tram services. When tram services were not running, (as there were no evening services) it was a fair walk to the Netham or similar departure points.

It is believed that the following service was transferred to Western National:-
Stroud - Tetbury - Malmesbury service in 1931: presumed that the Stroud - Malmesbury section given up and Malmesbury - Tetbury part incorporated into it.

Appendix 6

Map of routes

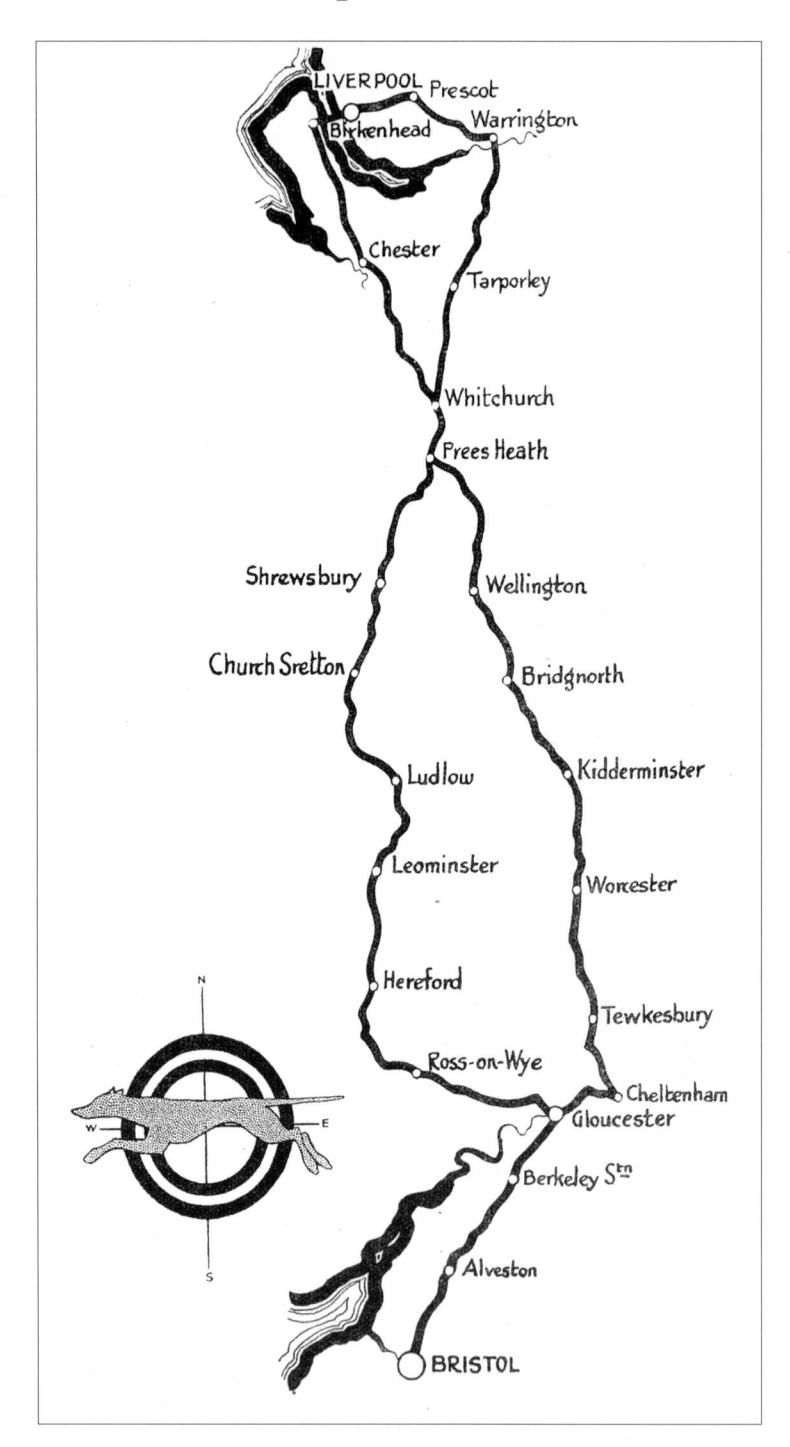

Map extract from the early nineteen thirties guide to Greyhound "Saloon Coach Services" showing the route(s) of the Liverpool to North Devon Coast express route over the Liverpool to Bristol section. There was a map shown against each service

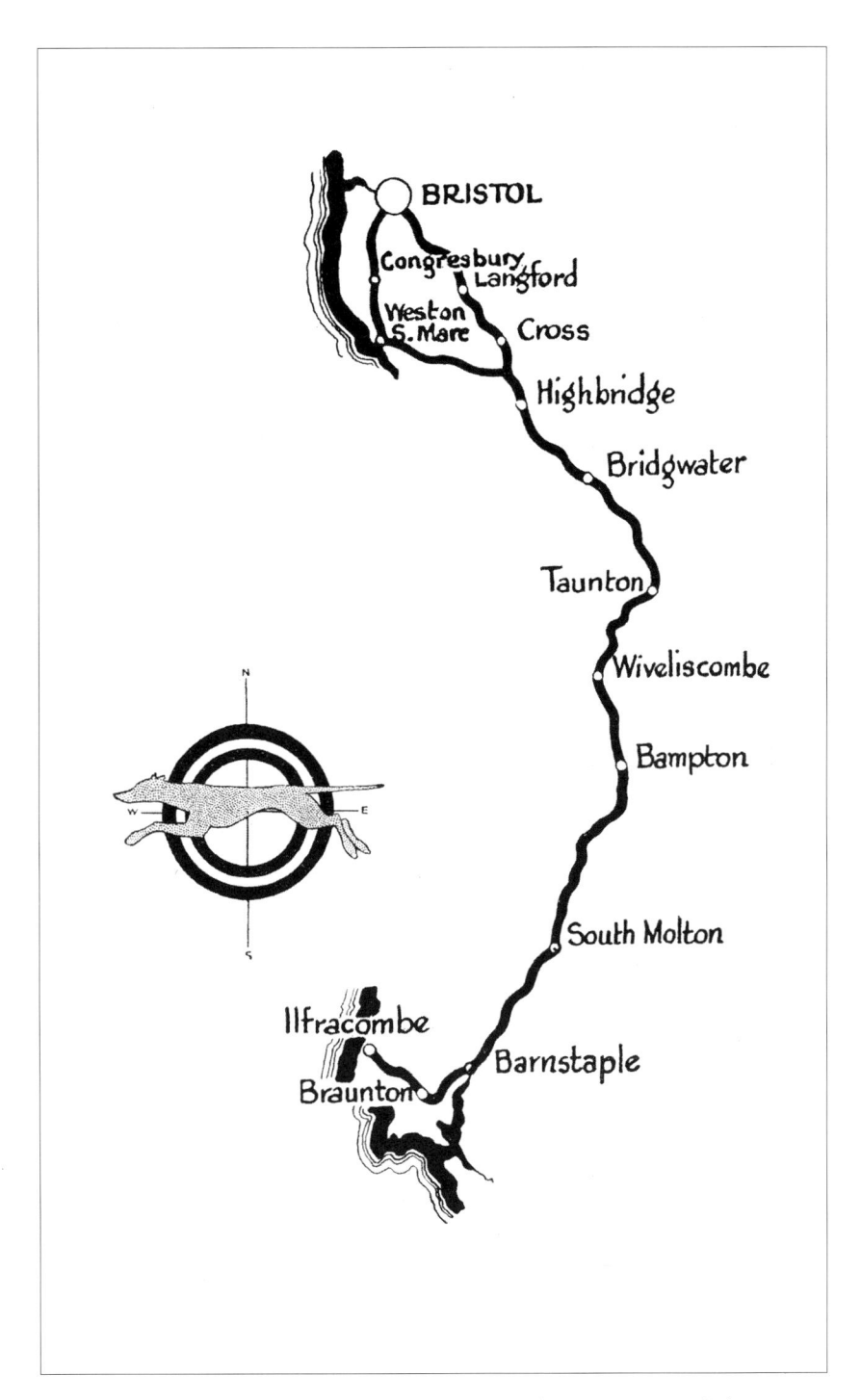

Continuation map for the Bristol to Ilfracombe section of the Liverpool to North Devon express service.

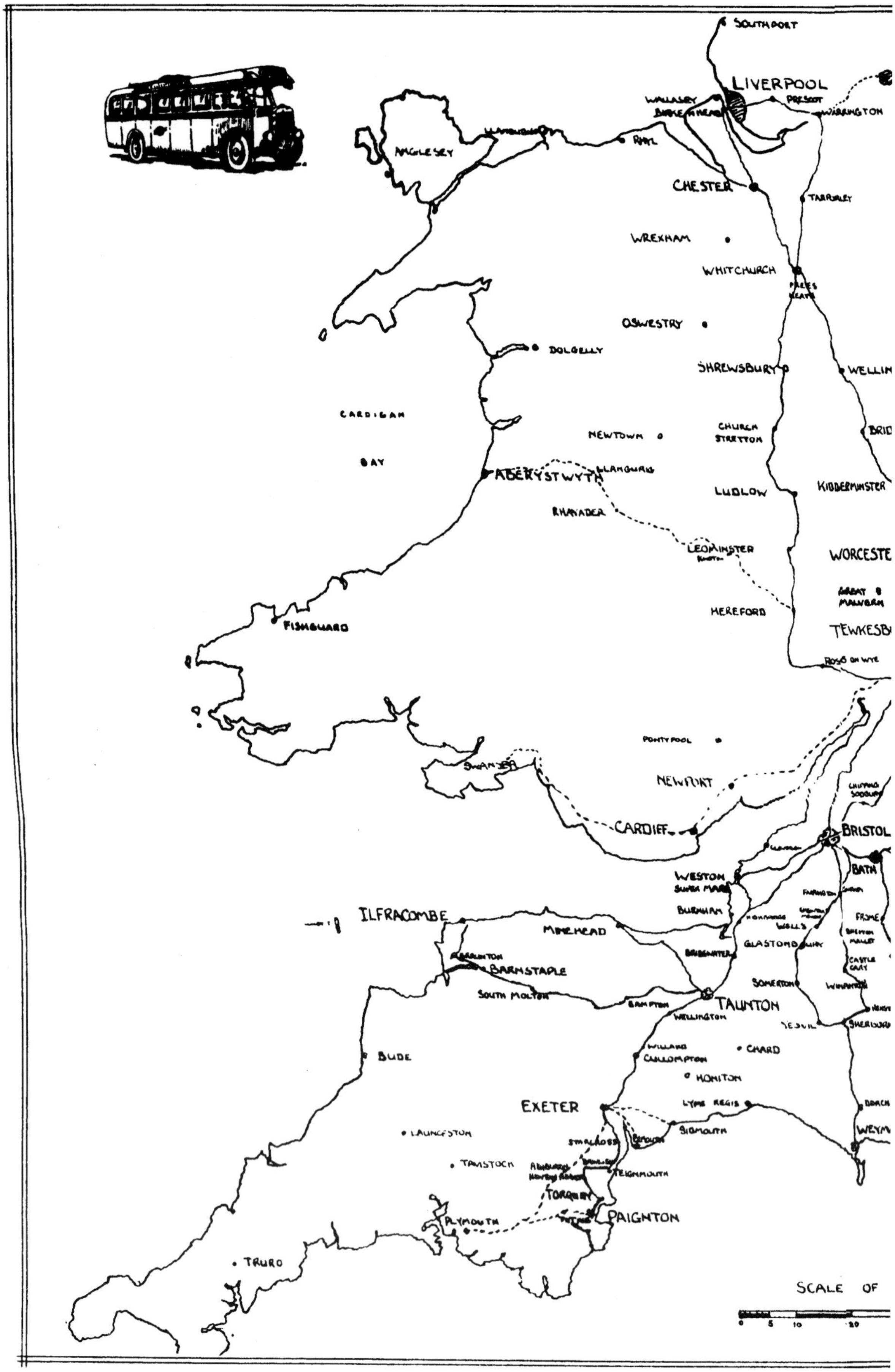
SOUTHPORT
LIVERPOOL
WALLASEY
PRESCOT
WARRINGTON
ANGLESEY
RHYL
CHESTER
TARPORLEY
WREXHAM
WHITCHURCH
OSWESTRY
DOLGELLY
SHREWSBURY
CARDIGAN
BAY
NEWTOWN
CHURCH
STRETTON
ABERYSTWYTH
LLANGURIG
RHAYADER
LUDLOW
KIDDERMINSTER
LEOMINSTER
WORCESTE
HEREFORD
TEWKESB
FISHGUARD
PONTYPOOL
SWANSEA
NEWPORT
CARDIFF
BRISTOL
BATH
WESTON
SUPER MARE
BURNHAM
ILFRACOMBE
MINEHEAD
WELLS
GLASTONBURY
FROME
BRIDGWATER
BARNSTAPLE
SOMERTON
SOUTH MOLTON
BAMPTON
TAUNTON
WELLINGTON
YEOVIL
SHERBORNE
BUDE
CHARD
CULLOMPTON
HONITON
LYME REGIS
EXETER
LAUNCESTON
SIDMOUTH
TAVISTOCK
TEIGNMOUTH
TORQUAY
PAIGNTON
PLYMOUTH
TRURO
SCALE OF
0
5
10
20

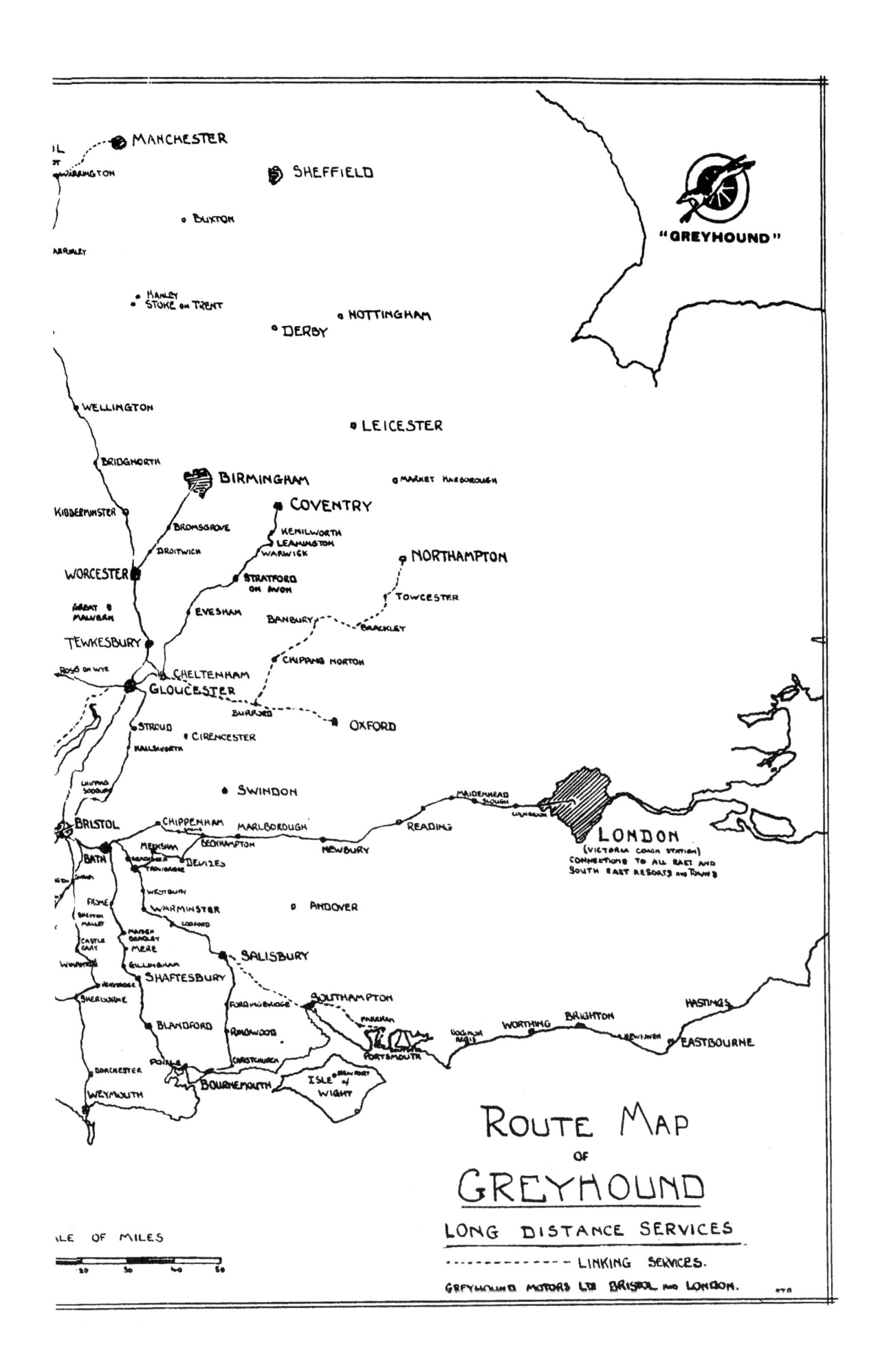

ROUTE MAP
OF
GREYHOUND
LONG DISTANCE SERVICES

---------- LINKING SERVICES.

GREYHOUND MOTORS LTD BRISTOL AND LONDON.

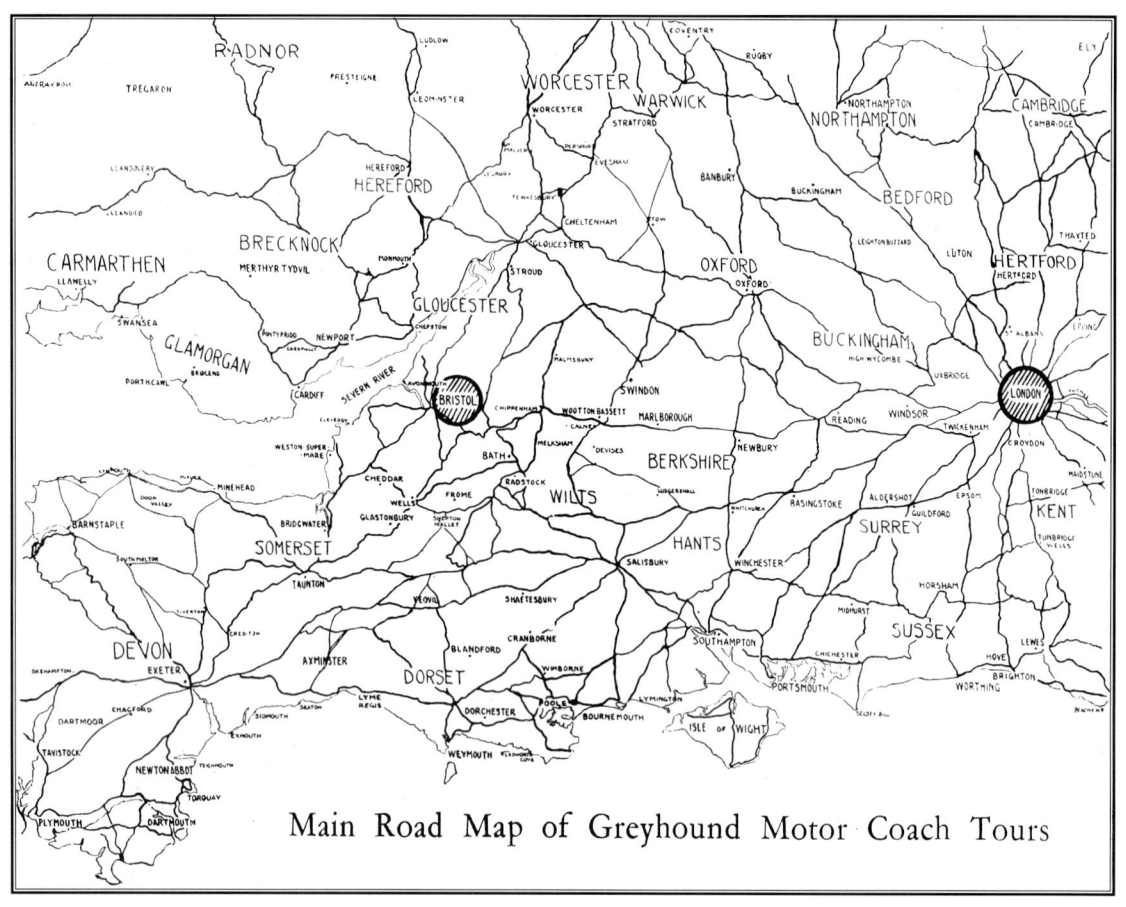

Main Road Map of Greyhound Motor Coach Tours

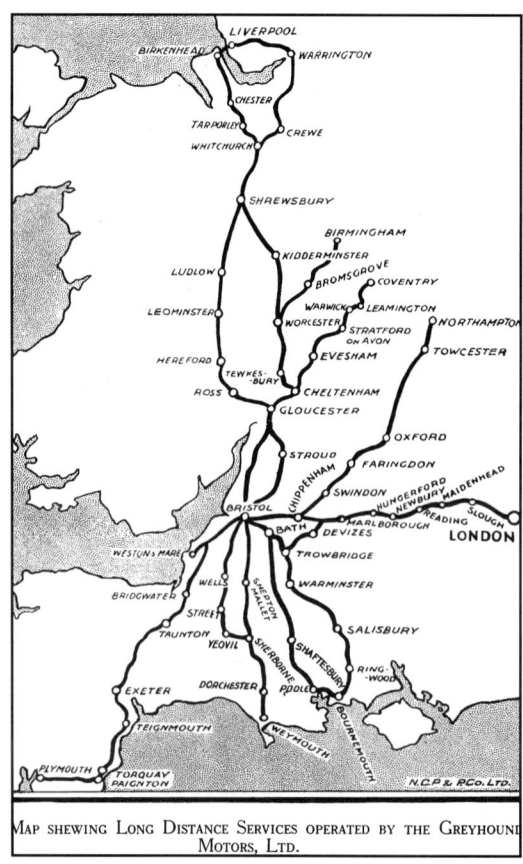

Map shewing Long Distance Services operated by the Greyhound Motors, Ltd.

Motor Coach Tours and Long Distance Services map from early 1930's Greyhound brochure.

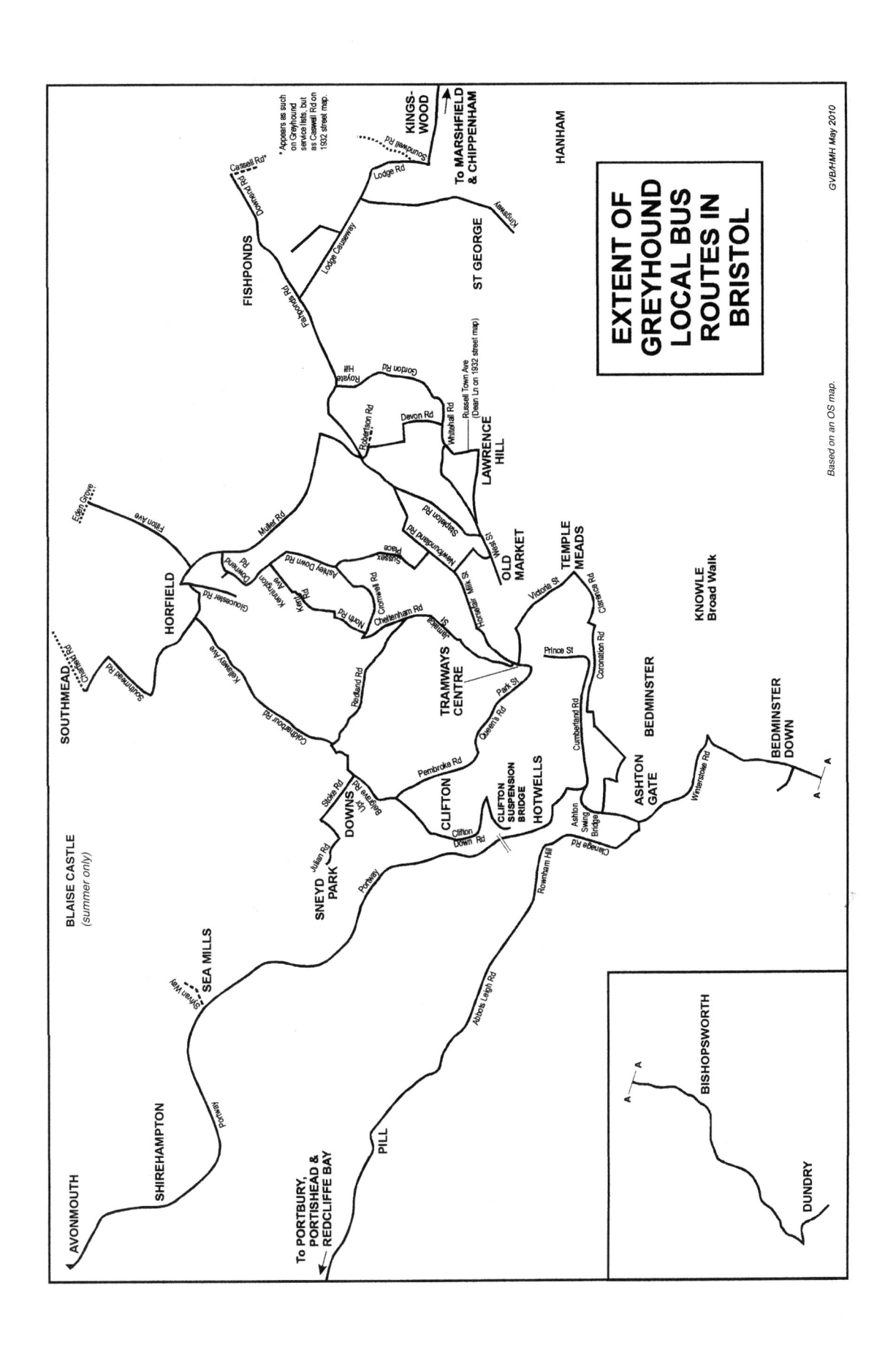

EXTENT OF GREYHOUND LOCAL BUS ROUTES IN BRISTOL

Appendix 7

The Organization of Long - Distance Coach Services
(reprint of 1934 Omnibus Magazine article)

THE OMNIBUS SOCIETY.

THE ORGANISATION

OF A

LONG DISTANCE COACH OPERATING COMPANY.

P A P E R

read before The Omnibus Society, by Mr.A.E.C.Bryant (Director and Traffic Manager of The Greyhound Motors Ltd., of Bristol and London) at a Meeting of the Society, held at The Institute of Marine Engineers, The Minories, London, E.C.3. on

Friday, December 9th, 1932, at 7.15 p.m.

The Omnibus Society,
    4, Wellington Road,
       Bow,
           LONDON, E.3.

Phone - East 4691.

Mr. Chairman, and Gentlemen,

May I first thank you, Mr. Chairman, for the opportunity afforded to me, by your Society, in reading this paper.

I am prefacing my Paper with a Commentary on the birth of, and advancement in the Industry, and am closing the same with remarks on the present situation as governed by the Road Traffic Act of 1930.

I have, for the purpose of avoiding a long statement as to the System of Operation, and Organisation, compiled a set of documents, as contained in the accompanying folder, each document being numbered to correspond with the marginal number as shown in the paper, and this will, I hope, be of assistance to the Members, in following my remarks and comments, so that when questions are asked upon the various parts of the paper, they may be confined to the particular point, under that reference number.

THE BIRTH OF LONG DISTANCE ROAD SERVICES.

Prior to 1925, travel as between Cities and Towns situated far apart was only available by Railway, except on special occasions when Motor Coach Tours were organised, and then primarily at week-ends. During 1924 these Motor Coach Tours had reached their zenith, and in that year my Company was looking round to find fresh 'ground to plough'. Having previously run special Tours to London by Motor Coach, we considered opening a daily guaranteed Service as between Bristol and London (despite the fact that at that time the speed limit was 12 miles per hour), and on February 11th, 1925, this initial route was opened with a once daily Service each way between the Terminal Points.

It is believed that this was the first daily Long Distance Service of 100 miles, to be operated in the Country, with a fixed Timetable and Fare Schedule, having 6d fares as between certain points, as a minimum.

The time taken over the journey at the opening of the route was 8 hours. There were many intermediate stages. The inauguration of this Service caused much comment throughout the Country, and in one paper, "The Bath Herald", under date November 14th, 1924, (prior to the opening of the Service), an article was published under the head-lines -

"TO LONDON BY 'BUS"
AN EXAMPLE NOT LIKELY TO BE FOLLOWED.

The writer of the article said:-

> "The success or otherwise of such a Service depended on the real need for the Service. It was inconceivable that the Public would travel, for instance, from Bristol to London, and make a journey lasting 8½ hours, when the same journey could be made by train in 2 hours. He was of the opinion that the promoters were unduly optimistic if they were depending on any material revenue in this direction. Possibly the promoters were anticipating deriving their revenue from short distance traffic between points en route, but, with the exception of, may be, a few miles of the road, nearly the whole of the route was covered by established Bus services which at the present time were amply sufficient for the public needs."

Page 1.

In Bristol, where the Service was commenced, the then Chief Constable (J. H. Watson Esq.,) whilst not opposing the Service, as a Service, openly stated to the Licensing Council that in his opinion the Service would not last six months, and that there would be no harm in giving it a trial, as no one would wish to go by road for such a long distance as Bristol to London - 115 miles.

Whilst this was the view on the one hand, other papers published statements such as the following:-

> "A new and important development in Motor Bus services is promised for the New Year - no less than a daily service to and from London and Bristol. Though there have been many Summer Services, we believe this guaranteed daily trip throughout the year will mark an innovation for this Country, in point of length. Application has been made to the various local authorities en route to pick up passengers, and generally, permission has readily been granted, the amenities the service will afford, being welcomed."

Prior to the opening of this initial Service, and during its infancy, my Company met with much opposition from various local bodies. The General Public, however, gave us ample encouragement to 'get on with the job', and shortly after the inception of the first "once daily" Service it was found necessary to run twice and then three times daily each way. This in spite of the fact that the Service was opened with Solid-Tyred vehicles, and which to-day would be looked upon with scorn.

Suffice it for me to say, that from this date (February, 1925), Long Distance road travel has spread throughout the Country, and has become an Industry of its own.

It has been claimed by some Operators that they were the pioneers of Long Distance travel, but whatever was the actual date of the birth of Road Travel (and it certainly was not later than February, 1925), this Industry has moved with rapid strides, and is now a material factor in the trade of this Country.

Indeed, the growth of the modern Long Distance

Coaching Industry has been as rapid and phenomenal as that of, say, Wireless. The two trades have, in fact, developed side by side.

The British Broadcasting Corporation have recently celebrated their tenth anniversary. We, of the Long Distance Motor Coaching Industry have yet three years to go to attain that distinction, and who shall say which will provide the more astounding comparison - the first "cats whisker" Crystal Receiver, and the modern Ultra Super-Heterodyne Set, or the first solid-tyred Long Distance Road Saloon and the super-deluxe Coach of 1935?

Since February, 1925, many Services have been opened by numerous Operators, to and from all parts of the Country, and the following are very material figures in support of the great strides which have been made in the linking up of main Cities and Towns, and the numerous villages not previously easily accessible by rail or road, as extracted from the first Annual Report of the Traffic Commissioners, covering the period January 1st 1931 to March 31st 1932, the figures quoted being for the year ended December 31st, 1931, in respect of Express Services only:-

Passenger Journeys.	32,821,381.
Passenger Receipts.	4,914,247.
Average Receipt per Passenger Journey.	35.93 pence.
Receipts from the conveyance of parcels, etc.	£6,689.
Gross Receipts - all sources.	£4,920,936.
Vehicle miles operated.	102,848,169.
Average Receipt per vehicle mile.	11.48 pence.

NOTE:

It is understood that approximately 80% of the figures above quoted relate specifically to Long Distance Services of at least 50 miles, single journey, and that included in such figures are some Services which are, in effect, Stage Carriages with fares of 1/- minimum and thereby classified as Express Carriages.

Page 3.

An example of the growth of the Industry is evidenced by the fact that in February, 1925, when my Company opened the Bristol - London route, one service daily only was operated, covering a daily mileage of approximately 230 miles. This grew to a three times daily service each way, and was extended to Weston-super-Mare, giving a daily mileage of approximately 850 miles.

In addition to these three services two other Operators have since come on the route, and they, as between them, operate five services a day with a mileage of about 1,100 miles daily, which, with my Company's service, covers approximately 2,000 miles per day, of passenger road transport over this one route, between Weston-super-Mare and London.

In like proportion most of the routes of other Operators have grown so that to-day the figures quoted in the Traffic Commissioners' Reports are a clear indication of the progress of the Industry.

The advancement has not been over smooth and concrete paths. The first serious obstacle with which my Company, (as pioneers) were faced, was that of the right to 'ply for hire' within the Metropolitan Area.

It was not, however, only in connection with the _right_ to operate with which my Company were concerned, but also with the development of the _system_ of operation, as shown by the trend of experience and the increasing desire of the public to "Travel by Road".

It was soon realised that some form of effective advertising (apart from the Press) must be organised.

With the decision that Coaches might only pick up booked passengers in the Metropolitan Area (viz., passengers booked 15 minutes prior to the advertised departure time of the Coach from its London terminal point) the first really organised appointment of Booking Agents was commenced. This was followed by the distribution in all parts of London and en route, of a two-colour Poster depicting the Coach and giving

Page 4.

full times and fares.

This Poster distribution had a very material effect on traffic, and resulted also in many enquiries for Agencies. I have been told, by the way, that certain of these Posters which were distributed in London in 1925 and 1926 may still be seen in some Hotels and Restaurants. Whether the retention of these is for sentimental reasons, or merely to avoid the expense of re-papering, I'm afraid I cannot say!

It was seen that existing Agents covered a comparatively small territory, and that it was essential to drive right home to the Public the fact that "it was possible to Travel by Road".

At the present time it seems amusing that people had to be told this. Our main concern now, is to keep before them the facilities offered by a well established form of Transport.

Parallel with the development of the Agency System was that of the appointment of authorised Caterers on route. My Company had already gathered considerable experience in this direction from the operation of Motor Coach Tours, and Cafes and Restaurants were soon appointed on route which our Conductors were instructed to recommend to their passengers, an arrangement which ensured that adequate refreshment facilities would always be available on the arrival of the Coach. Catering, as a branch of this Industry, has now extended to such a degree that establishments have been opened at most recognised halting places.

An experiment was made by the Company in 1927 and 1928, by the inclusion in their Service of Dining Saloons and this facility was advertised and run as a "Non Stop Service".

It should be mentioned here that this particular type of Coach provided Lavatory accommodation.

The scheme of providing meals on a road vehicle was, however, found to be impracticable, and as the Catering arrangements en route improved, the interior of these Coaches was suitably converted.

It was realised that close co-operation between the Operator and Agents was essential, particularly in regard to advance bookings during the Summer months. Incidents of duplication of seats were reported and it was found that in many instances Agents were booking seats and issuing Tickets without sending any advice to the appropriate Terminal Agent.

As a remedy in 1927 my Company's London Office was opened at 229, Hammersmith Road, and I believe that this was the first Office opened in the Metropolis by Provincial Coach Operators controlling their own Services, and the present system of Advice or Copy Tickets, and the issue of Advice Cards as given to passengers, booking an open date Return, was adopted.

When the success of the Bristol - London Service was assured, other Operators opened up Services and thereby facilities were offered to the Public in Coach Travel to many other parts of the Country, particularly from London. Connections were also made possible in a short space of time to practically all main Towns. Agencies for the purpose of Bookings were opened up and Motor Coach Travel really commenced as an Industry.

THE SYSTEM & OPERATION OF LONG DISTANCE SERVICES.
(AS APPLICABLE TO MY COMPANY).

FIRST AS TO THE BOOKING SIDE OF THE SYSTEM.

With services extending as far apart as:-

    London to Bristol and Weston.
    Liverpool to Paignton and Ilfracombe.
    Birmingham and Coventry to Paignton and Ilfracombe.
    Bournemouth and Weymouth to Bristol.
    Bath to Torquay and Paignton.

covering a very full and comprehensive list of Cities and Towns (as will be seen by the Route Map of the Company's services accompanying this paper), it was considered necessary to appoint Agents in all main Towns, and at the moment over 600 Agents and Agencies book for the Company's services on the terms and conditions set forth in the Company's Agency Agreement (Document No.34).

DOCUMENT NO.   The procedure to be adopted is as follows:-

1.   (a) The Agent books a passenger on the Ticket (which is written in triplicate).
The top copy is given to the passenger, the second copy sent to the Terminal Agent, (either by Coach, or post the same day). The third copy is retained by the Agent for audit purposes.

2.   (b) If a passenger makes a return booking, then a Return Ticket is issued covering both portions of the journey; but showing one half of the return fare on each portion, the appropriate advice copy being sent to the Terminal Agents.

3.& 4.   (c) If a passenger desires to leave open the date of travel for the return journey, the Agent issues to such passenger an advice card and envelope, addressed to the Terminal Agent, which, when received, guarantees a seat.

Page 7.

DOCUMENT NO.

5.
    (d) In the event of a passenger notifying the Conductor of a Coach or an Intermediate Agent of the date of return, the Conductor or Agent notifies the Terminal Agent on a Notification Sheet, and which acts as an advice the usual way.

6.
    (e) At the Terminal Offices of the Company the bookings are entered on a Coach Chart, showing the actual points of travel of <u>all booked passengers.</u>

    (f) When any chart indicates that the Coach is fully booked, notification is at once given by the Terminal Clerk to the Control Clerk at the Bristol Control Office, who arranges to duplicate that service.
Duplication in general is arranged from the nearest point where vehicles may be available for this purpose, thereby saving as much dead mileage as possible.

7.
    (g) When it is impossible, or impracticable to duplicate a service, for any reason, the Control Clerk immediately sends to all Agents an advice card to "stop bookings" on that particular service time.

8.
    (h) General Instructions to Agents, covering all Long Distance Services (which, of course, are subject to amendment from time to time) are issued in printed form, and which simplify the duty of the Agent.

TERMINAL AGENTS.

9.
    (a) The Terminal Agent, or Clerk, in all cases records the arrival and departure of all vehicles at his Terminal, by completing the Arrival and Departure Sheet provided by the Company for the purpose, thus assuring the regularity of service and efficient control

Page 8.

and is also a check on the Conductor's journey sheet.

(b) The Terminal Agent each week (or more often if convenient) sends to the Bristol Control Office, all duplicate or counterfoil advice copies of tickets, as received, after same have been entered on his Charts. (All advice cards or other Notifications are also returned).

These Tickets when received at the Head Office are entered in the Agency "Loose Leaf" Record Book and are dealt with as subsequently referred to.

AS TO THE CONDUCTORS' PART OF THE OPERATION.

Conductors are carried on all Long Distance Service coaches.

When a service is duplicated, one Conductor may in some instances be responsible for two or three coaches, (if the seating of a vehicle does not exceed 26 passengers) - but where possible all vehicles are allocated a separate Conductor.

The Conductor's duty is as follows:-

DOCUMENT NO.
10.
(a) To collect the Agent's ticket from the passenger, and in exchange issue a Coach ticket, showing the journey, and, in fact, all the details as given on the Agent's ticket.

(b) In no instance does a Conductor take from the passenger the return half of a ticket on the forward journey.

(c) Where a passenger travels, and has not pre-booked his ticket, the Conductor will issue a Coach ticket marked "Cash" similar to the ticket previously mentioned (Document No.10).

11.
(d) Where a cash passenger pays for a Return ticket on the coach, then the Conductor will issue a Coach Return ticket showing the full return

Page 9.

DOCUMENT NO.

fare on that one ticket, which when used on the return journey is defaced by centre clipping, and a single Coach Ticket issued in replacement.

12.
(e) Where through bookings are made from one service to another, or where arrangements have been made with other Operators, the Conductor will, (in addition to the Coach Ticket), issue to the passenger a Transfer Ticket. This Transfer Ticket also sets forth the full details given on the Agent's ticket.

(f) All Transfer Tickets are made out in duplicate, one copy of which is returned to the Head Office with the Conductor's way-bill, as verification of each transaction.

(g) All Coach Tickets issued by the Conductor are punched by him with the usual Bell Punch.

13.
(h) The way-bill to be completed by the Conductor shows the whole of the transactions made by him, and sets forth:-

    (a) The value of the Ticket tendered.
    (b) The value of the actual journey made on his particular coach.
    (c) The value of the Transfer Tickets (if any) made to other routes or services.

which columns when completed actually balance. The way-bill also gives a summary of the payment into the Office by the Conductor, whether by cash, vouchers, tickets, etc.

14.
(i) The Conductor also returns to the Office, a Transfer way-bill of all Transfer Tickets issued, corresponding with the details shown on the General way-bill.

Page 10.

DOCUMENT NO.

15. (j) In addition to the way-bill, it is the duty of the Conductor to keep a true record of the actual arrival and departure times of his Coach at each point on route, showing the delays, (if any), and the reasons therefor, and this is checked with the Terminal Agent's record sheet referred to (Document No.9).

(k) It is the duty also of all Conductors to call at the principal Agents on route, (which Agents are obtained as near as possible to the starting points) for the purpose of obtaining the advices of tickets booked, or other communications to the Terminal Offices.

AS TO LOST PROPERTY.

16. (1) Any Lost Property found on a Service Vehicle must be handed in by the Conductor at the Company's Office, immediately on return to Depot, and the appropriate form completed.

17. Passengers claiming Lost Property have to sign for such property on the form provided, paying the Statutory fees as defined in the section of the Road Traffic Act, details of which are also attached in extract form.

AS TO DRIVERS' DUTIES.

18. (a) The Driver's duty is mainly comprised of the control of his vehicle, and to give assistance to the Conductor in the loading of passengers' luggage. Labels are provided to all passengers (free of charge) when booking.

19. (b) The Driver is required at the end of each journey to complete a Motor Defects Sheet, giving details of any defect apparent during

Page 11.

DOCUMENT NO.

his journey, or of delays occasioned by involuntary stops, or otherwise.

(c) The Company's time-tables have always been compiled so that no Driver operates any coach longer than is reasonable, and the operation of the Road Traffic Act of 1930 has not affected this, by re-arrangement of duties.

Where possible Service Drivers are kept on the same route throughout the Season but with a variation of Conductors.

(d) No Driver is expected, or asked, to undertake any part of the cleaning or maintenance of his Coach, but all Drivers are picked men, with road experience and able to perform the usual running repairs.

20.
(e) In case of accidents (of any kind, and however small), all such are reported to the Company on the appropriate form. These forms must, in all instances, be **handed in at the conclusion of duty.**

In cases of material damage or serious personal injury the Driver (or his Conductor) must immediately telephone to the Garage Office at Bristol (a special line is kept for this purpose and such calls take precedence to any other calls) when the matter is immediately attended to and arrangements made for the replacement of the vehicle, and the transfer of passengers to another coach or Company's service.

GENERALLY.

(f) My Company being also the Operators of numerous Local Services, are in the happy position of being able to call upon Drivers

Page 12.

of experience to operate their Summer or Seasonal Long Distance Services, and the augmentation of such Services by duplication.

(g) All men engaged for Seasonal work are placed on Local routes; and at the end of the season are replaced by Drivers who have been operating on Long Distance routes for the Summer months.

My Company attribute their freedom from serious accidents, their reputation for Public safety, and the general regularity of their services, in a great measure, to their ability to retain the services of Long Distance Drivers or proved worth, by means of the opportunity of such retention, provided by a system of Local Bus Services in and around Bristol.

NOW AS TO THE OPERATIONS OF THE OFFICE STAFF.

On receipt of the Conductors' way-bills, charts, journey sheets, etc., all such are checked by the Receiving Clerk and the following procedure is adopted:-

(a) The way-bill is first checked with the copy Tickets issued, and the punch register; as regards the Summary of Passengers carried.

(b) The Agents' Tickets, and Transfer Tickets, are then verified by the Conductors' Exchange Coach Tickets as issued.

(c) Where cash is received by the Conductor, this is checked by the <u>cash</u> tickets issued, and cash paid in.

(d) Where Transfer Tickets are issued, the duplicate copies are checked as against the entries on the way-bills, and the amount shown as deducted from the Total way-bill.

<u>Page 13.</u>

DOCUMENT NO.

(e) The unused tickets are then checked as against the number debited to the Conductor, prior to his leaving the Depot, and if correct, the Ticket entry is verified, and the Conductor's box prepared for the next journey. A separate box is made up each time a Conductor returns to the Depot.

(f) The Conductors' copy coach tickets, and Agents' tickets then go to the Agency Department, where the Agents' tickets are

21. & 22.

recorded in the Agents' "Loose Leaf" Record Book, as having been used. These tickets are matched against the advice copies as already received from the Terminal Agents and as referred to in the Agency operations. Whichever copy of the ticket, (advice or passengers' portion), is first received is debited to the Agent at the end of the current month. This system always shows when any ticket booked by an Agent is outstanding, and also gives a record of the total amount of Agency bookings made by the Agent each particular month. The service letter in respect of each ticket booked is entered on the sheet in such Record Book and thus affords a direct check as to the actual routes upon which an Agent books.
Separate Records are used for Single and Return Tickets.

23.

(g) The way-bills when finally checked go to the Accountancy Department, where all such are entered into the Traffic Books, in respect of the appropriate route.

From these Traffic Books is made up the Waybill Monthly Analysis, showing the total receipts per month, the amount received by

Page 14.

DOCUMENT NO.

Cash by Agents' bookings, or from Transfer, or Foreign Tickets. **Note:** "Foreign Tickets" mean Tickets of other Operators or main Agencies.

Where a Conductor is over, or short, in his way-bill, this is recorded by means of debit or credit to the Conductors concerned, at the end of each month, and this Overs or

24. Short Analysis Sheet is posted on the Notice Board.

    (h) From such way-bills are also extracted the details of Transfers, made from one service to another, or from or to other joint, or linking services, and record the total transfers; and the details are then entered as against the respective routes.

25. These details are made monthly on the Analysis of Transfer form.

26.   (i) From the foregoing details an Analysis of Foreign Tickets is also made up, and these Tickets are invoiced to joint Operators, other Operators and main Agencies, whose tickets have been accepted on "Greyhound" services.

27.   (j) From the way-bills is also made up the numerous traffic records as to passengers, receipts, mileage, etc.

    (k) The records of passengers carried are compiled daily on a Monthly Passenger Summary in respect of each route, and the total number of passengers carried from one given Town to each other Town on the route, is thus indicated.

28.   (l) From these Town Sheets the Monthly Passenger Totals are compiled, showing the actual number of passengers travelling from any one

DOCUMENT NO.

    point to any other point, in either direction, and at the end of each year a similar Total Sheet is completed from these forms, giving the totals for the 12 months.

    By this method a direct check is made on the Traffics, rising or falling from any particular Town.

29. (m) Each month from the various book entries the Summary of Traffics Form is compiled, showing the Total seats available on the coaches employed; the total passengers carried on the route; the total vehicle journeys; the average passengers per journey; the total passenger receipts per mile, as also per passenger. This form shows the complete working of each route month by month, and annually.

30. (n) In like manner a Comparative Summary of Traffics is compiled, covering the material items, over a period of 3 years.

    (o) In the Company's Traffic Office is kept a Record Book showing the allocation of all vehicles, and by this procedure, all vehicles can be shown tracing their position, at any point, at any time, thus allowing easy duplication of services from the nearest possible point.

    From this book is also compiled a Schedule of
31. Extra or Special Coaches used on Long Distance Services, and these are charted daily on such Schedule against the route upon which engaged.

32. (p) From these Schedules is prepared a Summary of Special Coaches used for duplication and which shows, (against each route), monthly, the actual number of duplications made on the various days of the week, covering:-

Page 16.

DOCUMENT NO.

The Total for the month.

The Maximum used in any one day.

The Maximum used on any one journey.

This information is of paramount importance in presenting applications before the Traffic Commissioners, for additional vehicles or duplication of services.

33. (q) In addition to the foregoing forms there is also the Traffic Commissioners' own form, as required by them, (P.S.V.66B), which is more or less a duplication, (only framed differently), of the form used by my Company (Document No.29).

AS TO THE MAINTENANCE OF VEHICLES.

I think it would be as well to point out a few brief details relating to vehicles, and equipment necessary, for successfully operating Long Distance Motor Coach Services.

In the first instance, you will readily appreciate that the most suitable machines adapting themselves in every detail to meet the demands of the travelling public are essential.

My Company's knowledge of Public Service Vehicle operations, both Local and Long Distance, has enabled them to obtain a very high standard of efficiency; by obtaining chassis constructed upon the lines of sound practical experience and modern automobile engineering practice, in every detail, employing a full comprehensive system of maintenance, thus ensuring the maximum public safety.

Bodies designed upon the same principles and high class finish, deleting unnecessary frills, flounces and showmen's gadgets, and embodying all the comforts to be enjoyed by passengers availing themselves of Long Distance Motor Coach travel have always been their main objective.

Page 17.

As the subject of this paper is not intended to deal with any of the numerous problems relating to Maintenance systems, a few remarks touching upon the necessity for efficient organisation will suffice.

My Company carry out a very rigid system of inspection to all vehicles housed in its main Depot, every night. Vehicles sleeping out at Terminal Points are subject to the same routine when they return during the day, so that every machine in the Fleet is inspected once every 24 hours. Daily returns of inspection are checked to avoid the possibility of a vehicle being overlooked.

Drivers' Daily Motor Defect Reports are examined and cleared during the same period by an independent staff employed for this work, repairs or adjustments being signed for by the mechanic effecting same. It is essential that the Motor Defect Report Sheet be handed in for each vehicle daily, "All Correct" being stated where no defect is observed. A cross check is made between Daily Vehicle Inspection Sheets and Motor Defect Reports. This method entirely obviates the possibility of a machine "getting away" uninspected.

A like system is employed in the self-contained Maintenance Shops for pre-determined examinations, dock overhauls, complete overhauls, and painting.

All vehicles are due to leave the Running Sheds before commencing service at specially allocated times, a special "booking out and in" Sheet being kept for recording the actual times of departure and arrival; any vehicle commencing Service before or after schedule time will at once be detected.

Involuntary stops are negligible these days as will be shown by the following facts.

The route mileage covered by my Company's Long Distance Services is now 1,695 miles and for the period during the first nine months of this year approximately ONE MILLION miles were covered, no miles having been lost to

Page 18.

any Service and only seven involuntary stops occurred, viz.,

1. Radiator tube burst.
2. Two broken autovac suction pipes.
3. Four punctures.

a record which I am sure speaks for itself.

A Fleet Allocation Chart is kept for the purpose of obtaining at a glance the position or whereabouts of any particular vehicle in the Fleet, at any time, whether on Service, in the Running Sheds, or the Maintenance Shops.

GENERAL ROUTINE.

In addition to the System of Operation as outlined under the foregoing headings, there is of course the general routine:- Keeping in touch with Booking Agents, the supervision of outdoor Staff by Foremen and Inspectors, the organisation required in the preparation of applications before the various Commissioners as to Public Service Vehicle Licences, Road Service Licences, etc., attendances at Public Sittings and Appeals, and the entering of Objections to other services.

These matters although essentially material, are too numerous to be specifically outlined in the time allocated to me for this paper.

In an organisation such as this, a certain amount of elasticity must, of necessity, be allowed in dealing with the requirements of the general public and conforming to the Provisions of the Road Traffic Act and Statutory Orders.

THE PRESENT SITUATION AS GOVERNED BY THE ROAD TRAFFIC ACT.

Prior to the Road Traffic Act of 1930 it was not necessary for an Operator of Long Distance Services to prove to a Licensing Authority the need for a new service, or the continuance of a then existing service, by the production of Traffic Statements and Analysis, but such Authorities, although very reticent in granting Licences, were more or less concerned with the protection of local services, particularly as to fares, and conformity with local regulations.

I have already referred to one of the main difficulties experienced in the early days, viz., the question of plying for hire, and it was no doubt consequent upon the chaos which was then made apparent by the inadequacy of the Authorities to deal with the question, as also the putting on to the road of services which did not supply a public demand, and in many instances the particular class of vehicle used, that the Road Traffic Act of 1930 was born.

Whatever the cause, it became apparent that with the development of passenger road traffic the need of more stringent control was necessary to put the Motor Coach Industry on a proper basis, and although the measures adopted have been, and still are, considered to be in some cases very drastic, by the discontinuance of services and the Regulations enforced by the Ministry through the Commissioners, yet at the same time, good, will I am sure, come from it, and all services which warrant their existence will continue, if operated in the interest of the public.

In my opinion any service which supplies a public need, and is conducted on equitable lines, will stand the strain, and continue as a source of revenue to the Operator; and in this respect the necessity of co-ordination of services is of paramount importance.

No Operator can, in his own interest, or that of the public, have for his Primary object the combating of another service, losing sight of the necessity of supplying a public demand, and these points are ever before the watchful eyes of the Commissioners when dealing with Applications for Road Service Licences.

The difficulties which have been experienced by Operators have also been apparent to the Traffic Commissioners, and in the Official Report by one of the Commissioners, he stated:-

> "I desire to acknowledge the very great assistance which I have received from those engaged in the Transport Industry, and to express my appreciation of the spirit of friendly co-operation with which they have endeavoured to overcome the inevitable difficulties which arose during the first years working of the procedure under the Road Traffic Act. There has been manifested a general tendency to recognise that such difficulties were temporary, and that although control may be irksome, it brings with it advantages and benefits which greatly outweigh the disadvantages."

With these facts before us, each Operator must "be practical" and strive to attain the highest efficiency, adapting his organisation to meet the ever changing conditions as hereby controlled.

Appendix 8

Tickets

A selection of local and express tickets.

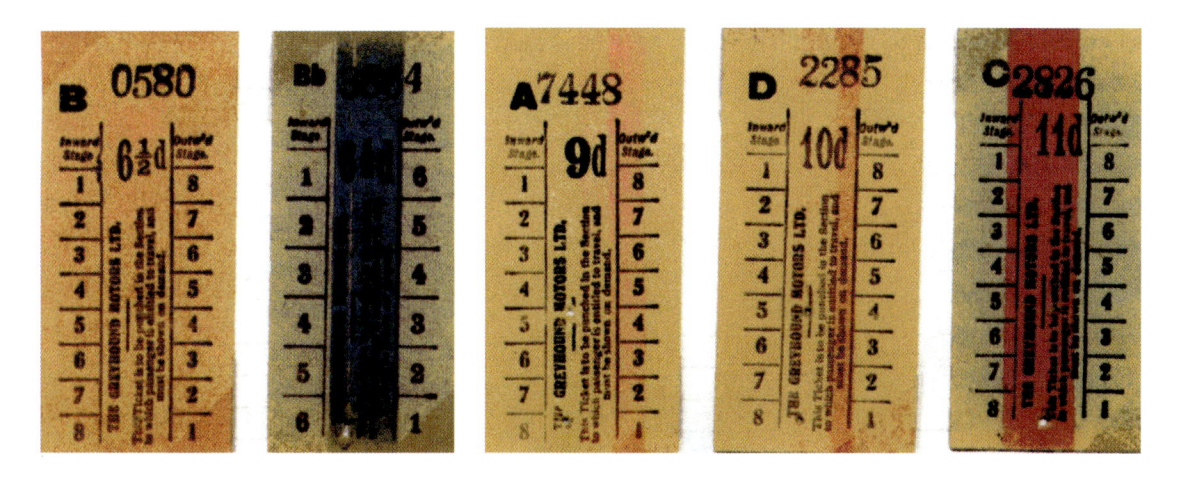

The above tickets are probably from the earliest period, 1921 onwards.

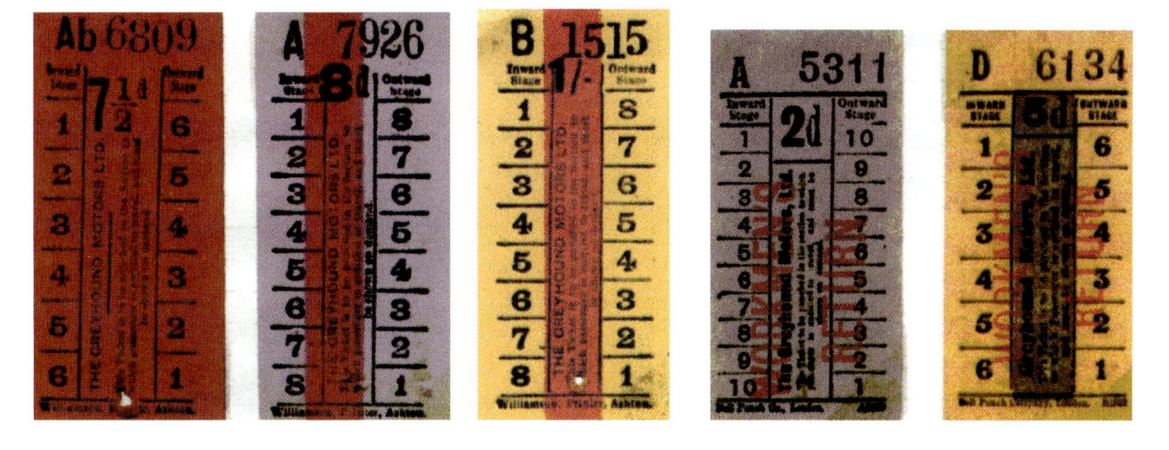

Williamson tickets, possibly up to the takeover by Bristol Tramways in 1928.

From 1924 until the late 1930s it is assumed that Greyhound used the same type of tickets as the Tramways, as above.

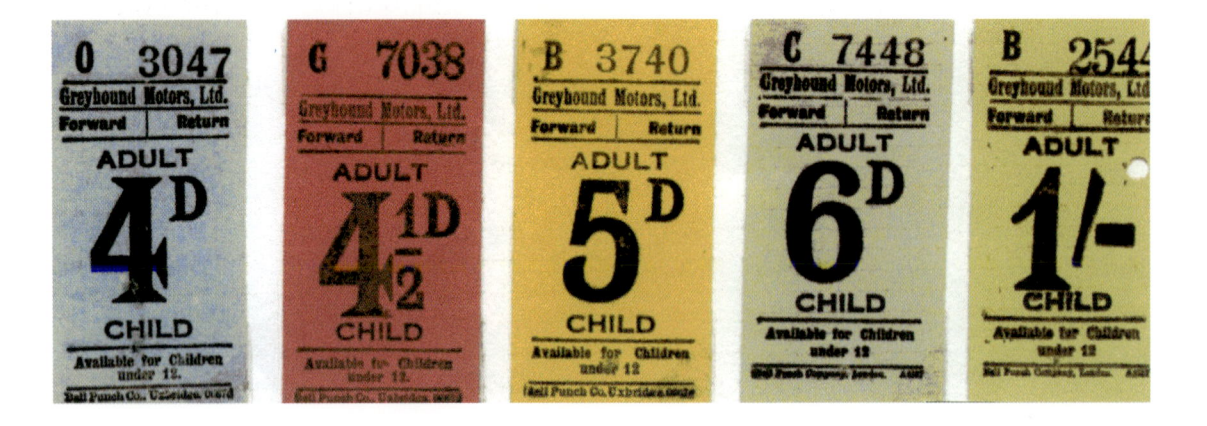

These tickets were probably in use by Greyhound from 1928 until absorption by The Tramways in 1936.

This is believed to be one of the earliest Greyhound express tickets, circa. 1925/1926.

The Hammersmith address at the top of this ticket indicates that Hammersmith was still the London terminus when this ticket was in use.

Two sides of express ticket 48654.

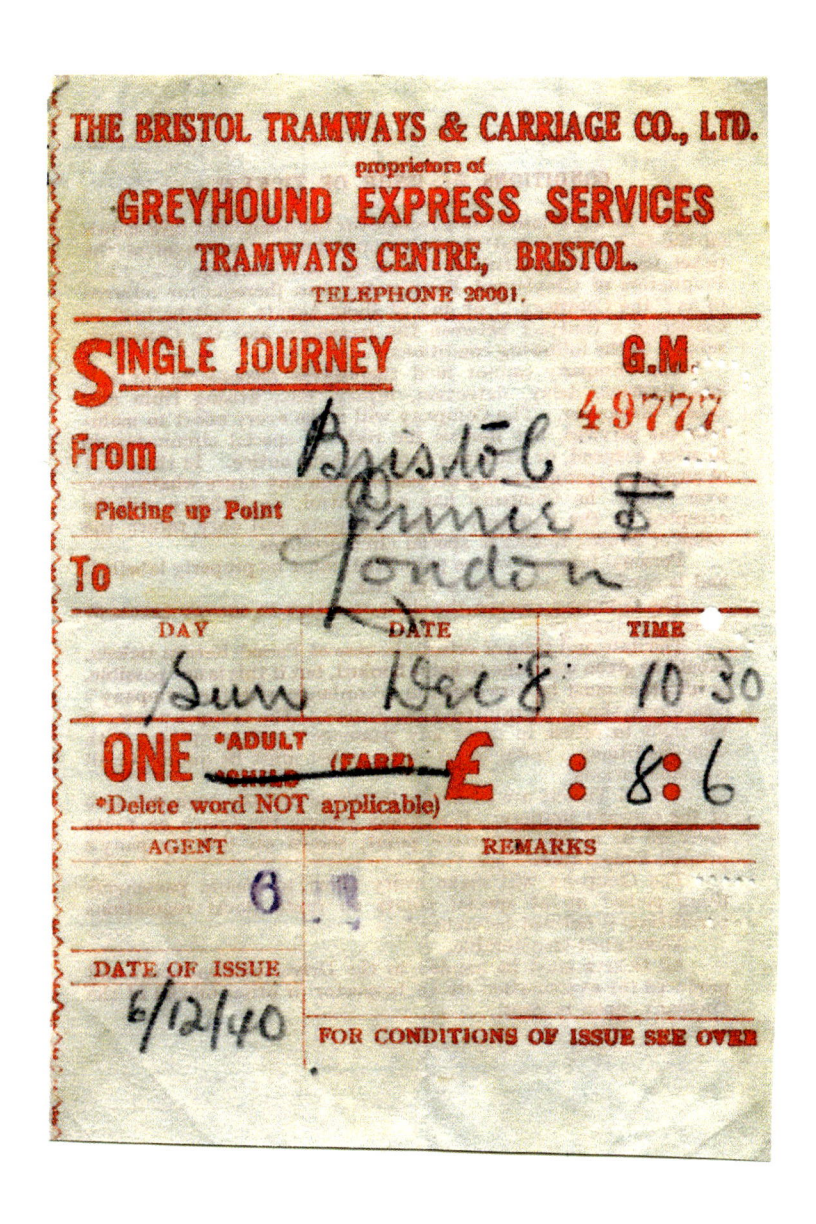

A Greyhound express ticket from 1940, after the Greyhound company had been fully absorbed into the Bristol Tramways Company.

Appendix 9

Timetables and leaflets.

A selection of leaflets, timetable covers, and timetables.

Dated 1921, this leaflet advertising a football match between Bristol and Reading also advertises the services of Greyhound Motors. Inside the leaflet were details of the two teams players.

The cover of an early booklet advertising a range of motor coach excursions provided by the Greyhound Company from Bristol in the early nineteen twenties. Inside was a comprehensive description of tours to places as far apart as Worcester, Stratford-on-Avon, Salisbury, Bournemouth and Minehead

The cover of a guide to Greyhound "Saloon Coach Services", probably from the early nineteen thirties, detailing a range of express services and holiday tours, including detailed points of interest to be seen en-route.

AMENDED WINTER SERVICE until further notice.

Time Table *and* Special Reduced Fares Single & Return.

THE GREYHOUND MOTORS, LTD.,

Express Saloon Coach Service

TO AND FROM BRISTOL & LONDON

Via Bath, Chippenham, Calne. | Beckhampton, Marlboro', Hungerford.
Bath, Trowbridge, Devizes | Newbury, Reading and Maidenhead.

THRICE DAILY—*(Sundays Included)*—**THRICE DAILY.**

The Amended Service will commence **SUNDAY, DEC. 23rd, 1928,** and continue until further notice.

GENERAL INFORMATION AND REGULATIONS.

LUGGAGE. A Suitcase is allowed Free to each Passenger, which is carried at the Owner's Risk.

RETURN FARES. A Return Ticket is available to return at any period, and Passengers are advised to inform the Bristol or London Office AS EARLY AS POSSIBLE of their Return Instructions, otherwise a Seat cannot be guaranteed.

For Complete Regulations see the Company's Official Time Table.

Issued by the Operators :— 'Phone 5800 Bristol.   OFFICIAL BOOKING AGENCY :—

The Greyhound Motors Ltd
5, St. Augustines Place
COLSTON STREET · BRISTOL

and

London Office: 229 Hammersmith Road,
'Phone: Riverside 4273.   London, W.6.

LODGE & SON, WEST ST. BRISTOL.

1928 leaflet including time and faretable for the Bristol to London service.

DAILY TIME TABLE
(SUNDAYS INCLUDED).

(CANCELS ALL PREVIOUS LISTS.)

From BRISTOL Read Down.			STOPPING and FARE STAGES.	From LONDON Read Up.		
DEPART				**ARRIVE**		
a.m.	a.m.	p.m.		p.m.	p.m.	p.m.
8.45	11.0	4.0	*BRISTOL (Prince Street) ...	3.20	6.45	10.20
9.25	11.40	4.40	*BATH (Top of Milsom Street)	2.40	6.5	9.40
10.6	—	5.21	*CHIPPENHAM (Market Place)	1.59	—	8.59
10.23	—	5.38	*CALNE ("Lansdowne Arms")	1.42	—	8.42
—	12.8	—	BRADFORD-ON-AVON (The Bridge)	—	5.37	—
—	12.18	—	*TROWBRIDGE (The "George" Hotel)	—	5 27	—
—	12 36	—	MELKSHAM (The Square) ...	—	5 9	—
—	12 58	—	*DEVIZES (The "Bear" Hotel)	—	4 47	—
10.43	1.23	5.58	BECKHAMPTON (Race Stables)	1.22	4.22	8.22
11.4	1.44	6.19	*MARLBOROUGH (Town Hall)	1.1	4.1	8'1
11.35	2.15	6.50	Arrive *HUNGERFORD (The 'Bear' Hotel) Depart	12.30	3.30	7.30
11.55	2.35	7.10	Depart „ „ Arrive	12.10	3.10	7.10
12.21	3.1	7.36	*NEWBURY (The Broadway) ...	11 44	2.44	6.42
12.59	3.39	8.14	THEALE	11.6	2.6	6.6
1.16	3.56	8.31	*READING (Wokingham Rd. Junct.)	10.49	1.49	5.49
1.52	4.32	9.7	*MAIDENHEAD (The 'Bear' Hotel)	10.13	1.13	5.13
2.9	4.49	9.24	*SLOUGH (The 'Crown' Hotel) ...	9.56	12.56	4.56
2.20	5.0	9.35	*COLNBROOK (The 'George' Hotel)	9.45	12.45	4.45
2.44	5.24	9.59	HOUNSLOW (The Broadway)	9.21	12.21	4.21
3.5	5.45	10.20	*HAMMERSMITH (London Office, 229 Hammersmith Road, W.6)	9.0 a.m.	12.0 noon	4.0 p.m.
ARRIVE						**DEPART**

* Regular Stopping Stages—at other Stages Coaches stop "On Request" only.
The above times are approximate only.

OTHER REGULAR DAILY LONG-DISTANCE SERVICES BY "GREYHOUND" COACHES :—

	FARES	
	Single	Return
BRISTOL and BOURNEMOUTH.		
Via Bath, Trowbridge, Westbury, Salisbury and Ringwood ...} Via Bath, Frome, Gillingham, Shaftesbury and Blandford ...}	7/6	12/6
BRISTOL, TORQUAY and PAIGNTON.		
Via Bridgwater, Taunton, Exeter, Teignmouth and Newton Abbot ...	8/6	14/6
COVENTRY, EVESHAM, GLOUCESTER, BATH, BRISTOL. TORQUAY and PAIGNTON	16/6	27/6

Timetable from the 1928 leaflet showing popular fares.

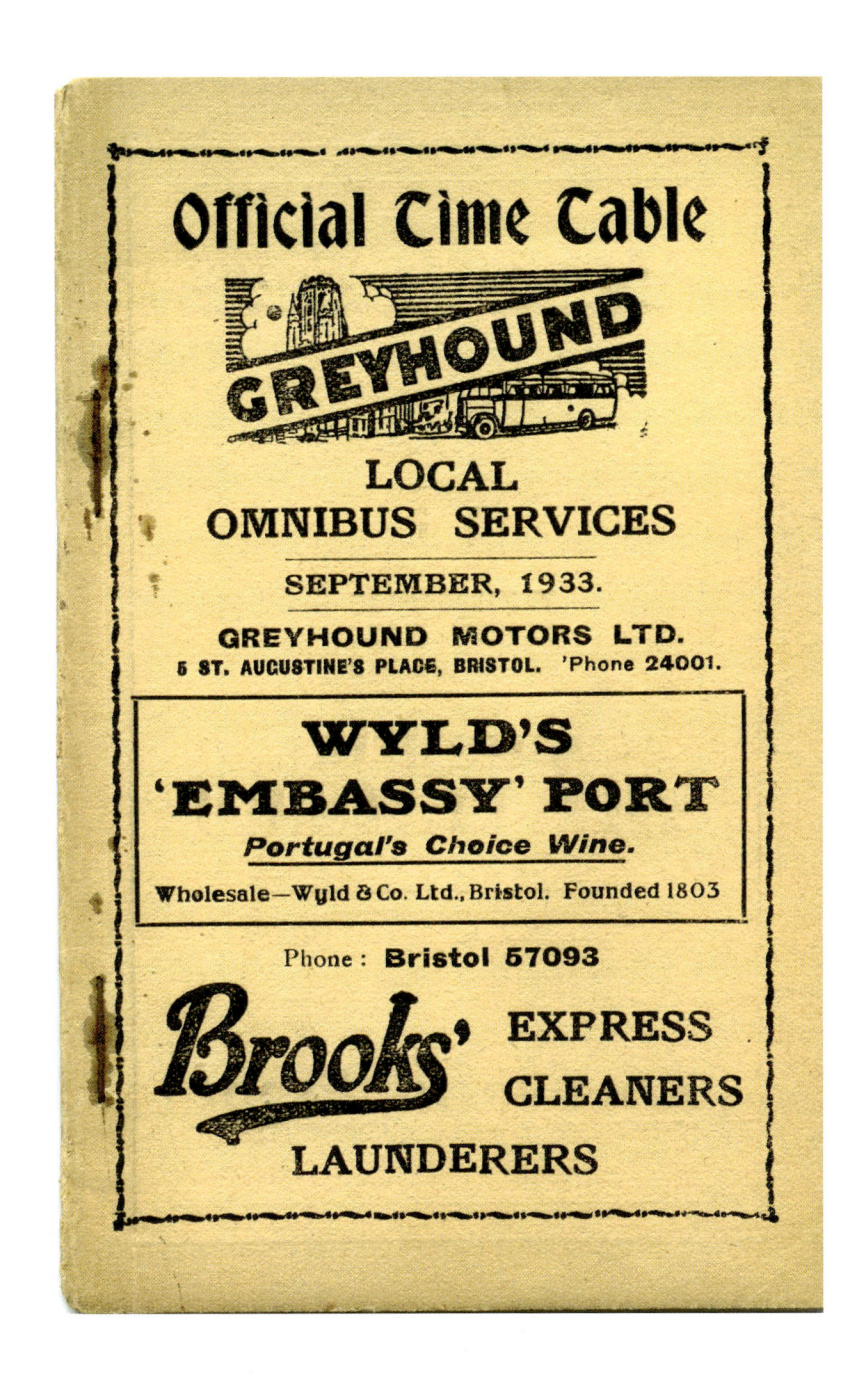

Cover of a 1933 local bus service timetable.

SERVICE 82

OLD MARKET, EASTVILLE, FISHPONDS (Causeway) and ST. GEORGE (Kingsway) or KINGSWOOD (Soundwell Rd.)

SUNDAYS.

	p.m.	p.m.	p.m.	p.m.	p.m.	p.m.	p.m.		p.m.	p.m.	
Old Market	1 40	1 50	2 0	2 10	2 20	2 30	2 40		10 10	10 20	—
Eastville (Robertson Road)	1 54	2 4	2 14	2 24	2 34	2 44	2 54		10 24	10 34	—
Fishponds Road (Causeway)	2 2	2 12	2 22	2 32	2 42	2 52	3 2	Then from Old Market every 10 mins. to Eastville and Thicket Avenue and 20 mins. to St. George (Kingsway) or Kingswood (Soundwell Road) until	10 32	10 42	—
Thicket Avenue	2 6	2 16	2 26	2 36	2 46	2 56	3 6		10 36	10 46	—
Two Mile Hill	—	2 20	—	2 40	—	3 0	—		10 40	—	—
St. George (Kingsway)	—	2 23	—	2 43	—	3 3	—		10 43	—	—
Kingswood (Soundwell Road)	2 14	—	2 34	—	2 54	—	3 14		—	—	10 54

	p.m.	p.m.	p.m.	p.m.	p.m.	p.m.	p.m.	p.m.	p.m.	p.m.	p.m.	p.m.		p.m.
Kingswood (Soundwell Road)	—	—	—	—	—	2 24	—	2 44	—	3 4	—	3 24	Then to Old Market every 20 mins. from St. George (Kingsway) or Kingswood (Soundwell Road) and 10 mins. from Thicket Avenue and Eastville until	—
St. George (Kingsway)	—	—	—	—	—	—	2 35	—	2 55	—	3 15	—		9 55
Two Mile Hill	—	—	—	—	—	—	2 38	—	2 58	—	3 18	—		9 58
Thicket Avenue	—	—	—	—	—	2 32	2 42	2 52	3 2	3 12	3 22	3 32		10 2
Fishponds Road (Causeway)	—	—	—	—	—	2 36	2 46	2 56	3 6	3 16	3 26	3 36		10 6
Eastville (Robertson Road)	1 44	1 54	2 4	2 14	2 24	2 34	2 44	2 54	3 4	3 14	3 24	3 34	3 44	10 14
Old Market	1 57	2 7	2 17	2 27	2 37	2 47	2 57	3 7	3 17	3 27	3 37	3 47	3 57	10 27

	p.m.	p.m.	p.m.	p.m.	p.m.	p.m.	p.m.
Kingswood (Soundwell Road)	10 4	—	10 24	—	10 40	—	10 55
St. George (Kingsway)	—	10 15	—	10 35	—	10 45	—
Two Mile Hill	—	10 18	—	10 38	—	10 48	—
Thicket Avenue	10 12	10 22	10 32	10 42	10 48	10 52	11 3
Fishponds Road (Causeway)	10 16	10 26	10 36	10 46	10 52	10 56	11 7
Eastville (Robertson Road)	10 24	10 34	10 44	10 54	11 0	11 4	11 15
Old Market	10 37	—	—	—	—	—	—

JOINT SERVICE—operated by Greyhound Motors Ltd. and the Bristol Tramways & Carriage Co., Ltd.

SERVICE 82.
FARES.

FROM \ TO	Old Market Street	Croyden Street	Devon Road	York Road (Belle Vue Rd.)	Eastville	Ridgeway Road	Fishponds Rd. (Causeway)	Thicket Avenue	Two Mile Hill or Cossham Hospital	Kingswood (Soundwell Rd.)
Old Market Street	—	1½d.	2d.	2d.	2d.	3d.	3½d.	4½d.	5d.	5d.
Croyden Street	1½d.	—	1½d.	1½d.	1½d.	2½d.	3d.	4d.	4½d.	5d.
Devon Road	2d.	1½d.	—	1d.	1d.	2d.	2½d.	3½d.	4d.	4½d.
York Road (Belle Vue Road)	2d.	1½d.	1d.	—	1d.	2d.	2½d.	3½d.	4d.	4½d.
Eastville	2d.	1½d.	1d.	1d.	—	1½d.	1½d.	2½d.	3d.	3½d.
Ridgeway Road	3d.	2½d.	2d.	2d.	1½d.	—	1½d.	2d.	2½d.	3d.
Fishponds Road (Causeway)	3½d.	3d.	2½d.	2½d.	1½d.	1½d.	—	1d.	1½d.	2d.
Thicket Avenue	4½d.	4d.	3½d.	3½d.	2½d.	2d.	1d.	—	1d.	1½d.
Two Mile Hill or Cossham Hospital	5d.	4½d.	4d.	4d.	3d.	2½d.	1½d.	1d.	—	1d.
Kingswood (Soundwell Road)	5d.	5d.	4½d.	4½d.	3½d.	3d.	2d.	1½d.	1d.	—

WORKMEN'S FARES.

	Return		Return
Old Market and Kingswood	7d.	Old Market and York Road (Belle Vue Road)	2½d.
Old Market and Fishponds (Causeway)	5d.	Eastville and Kingswood	5d.
Old Market and Eastville	3d.		

All Buses arriving at a Terminus before 8 a.m. carry Passengers at Workmen's Fares.
The Return Journey may be made at any time during the day of issue.

Sample pages from the 1933 local bus service leaflet showing service 82 times and fares.

The cover of the 1934 timetable for both long distance and City services. On 1st January 1936 the company was fully absorbed into The Bristol Tramways and Carriage Company.

Cover of the summer 1970 timetable showing the opening of the M4 motorway between Bristol and London. On the next page are details of the Weston-super-Mare Bristol timetable and faretable: note that the journeys operating entirely via the A4 take almost 5 and a half hours, compared with the 8 hours of the first pioneering journeys, and the 6 hours 20 minutes shown in the 1928 timetable.

WESTON-SUPER-MARE · BRISTOL · BATH · MARLBOROUGH · LONDON
BRISTOL · SWINDON · LONDON

TABLE 1

"BRISTOL — GREYHOUND"

Daily — 17th May, 1970 to 10th October, 1970

							FSu	S	F		FS
WESTON-SUPER-MARE, Bus Station	....	....	....	....	1145	1430	....	1430	....	1630	....
Congresbury, Post Office	....	....	....	....	1207	1452	....	1452	....	1652	....
BRISTOL, Coach Stn., Marlborough Street arr	....	....	....	....	1235	1520	....	1520	....	1720	....
BRISTOL, Coach Stn., Marlborough Street dep	0700	0830	1130	1130	1245	1530	1530	1530	1730	1730	2330
Kingswood, opposite Park Lay-by	....	....	....	....	....	....	1542	....	....	....	....
Brislington, 7 Grove Park	0710	0840	1140	1140	NON-STOP via A420, A4 and M4	1540	....	1540	....	1740	2339
Keynsham, Church	0716	0846	1146	1146		1546	....	1546	....	1746	2343
Saltford, Crown Hotel	0722	0852	1152	1152		1552	....	1552	....	1752	2348
Newton St. Loe, Globe Inn	0726	0856	1156	1156		1556	....	1556	....	1756	2352
Bath, Bus Station, Manvers Street	0740	0910	1210	1210		1610	....	1610	1800	1810	2359
Batheaston, Petrol Station, Five Ways	0750	0920	1220	1220		1620	....	1620	....	1820	0008
Box, Post Office	0757	0927	1227	1227		1627	....	1627	....	1827	0015
Rudloe Manor, R.A.F.	0801	0931	1231	1231		1631	....	1631	....	1831	0019
Pickwick, opposite Pickwick Stores	0804	0934	1234	1234		1634	....	1634	....	1834	0022
Chippenham, Bus Terminal, The Wharf	0813	0943	1243	1243		1643	1634	1643	1832	1843	0031
Lyneham, Edmonds Garage	....	....	....	....		....	1700	....	LONDON AIRPORT SPECIAL via A4 & M4	....	....
Wootton Bassett, Borough Arms	....	....	....	....		....	1710	....		....	....
Swindon Bus Station arr	....	....	....	....		....	1725††	....		....	....
Swindon Bus Station dep	....	....	....	....		....	1740††	....		....	....
Swindon, Queen's Drive, The Bulldog	....	....	....	....		....	1743††	....		....	....
Swindon, Queen's Drive/Ripon Way	....	....	....	....		....	1745††	....		....	....
Calne, The Strand	0827	0957	1257	1257		1657	NON-STOP via A4 and M4	1657		1857	0043
Beckhampton, Race Stables	0841	1011	1311	1311		1711		1711		1911	0056
Marlborough, opposite Good Fare Cafeteria arr	0854	1024	1324†	1324†		1724		1724		1924	0109
Marlborough, opposite Good Fare Cafeteria dep	0909	1039	1339	1339		1754		1754		1954	0119
Hungerford, opposite Bear Hotel	0929	1059	1359	1359		1814		1814		2014	0139
Newbury, Thames Valley Bus Shelt. opp. St. Mary's Ch.	0948	1118	1418	1418		1833		1833		2033	0156
Thatcham, opposite Lester's Garage	0955	1125	1425	1425		1840		1840		2040	0202
Theale, Theale Motor Works	1013	1143	1443	1443		1858		1858		2058	0220
Reading, Bus Station, Station Hill arr	1022‡	1152‡	1452	1452		1907‡		1907		2107	0229
Reading, Bus Station, Station Hill dep	1030●	1200●	1500●	1500		1915●		1915		2115	0235
Maidenhead, Bus Station	NON-STOP via A4 and M4	NON-STOP via A4 and M4	NON-STOP via A4 and M4	1531		NON-STOP via A4 and M4		1946		2146	0306
Slough, Post Office				1548				2003		2203	0319
Colnbrook Turning, opposite The Plough				1557				2012		2212	0328
London Airport, Heath Row, Central Area				....				....	2125	....	....
London Airport, opposite North Gate Entrance				1606				2021	....	2221	0335
Great West Road, Lampton Cross Roads				1619				2034	....	2234	0343
Chiswick, Heathfield Terrace				1634				2049	....	2249	0353
Hammersmith, Latymer Court				1644				2059	....	2259	0401
LONDON, Victoria Coach Station	1145■	1315	1615	1659	1700□	2030	2025	2114	2210	2314	0414

For details of through and connecting services beyond London to the South and East Coasts, ask for Leaflet CS.1.

CODE

FSu—Fridays and Sundays only. (Operates additionally on Monday, 25th May and Monday, 31st August).

F—Fridays only.

S—Saturdays only.

FS—Fridays and Saturdays only.

†—Change coaches for Swindon, Oxford and Intermediate points to London (see Table 2).

††—Passengers cannot be set down in Swindon.

●—Passengers cannot be picked up in Reading.

■—Continues to Southend-on-Sea on Sundays only arr. 1441.

□—Continues to Southend-on-Sea arr. 2026 (Not 10th October).

‡—This service connects at Reading with "Thames Valley" Service "B" as follows:—

Reading, Bus Station	0700		2200
Maidenhead, Bus Station	0740		2240
Slough, Post Office, High Street	0757	and	2257
Colnbrook, opp. George Hotel	0807		2307
London Airport, Blue Star Garage	0816	hourly	2316
Great West Road, Lampton Cross Roads	0829	until—	2329
Chiswick, Robin Hood	0844		2344
Hammersmith, Latymer Court	0851		2351

SEATS NOT BOOKABLE, PASSENGERS PAY ON THAMES VALLEY BUS.

WESTON-SUPER-MARE · DEVIZES · SWINDON · OXFORD · LONDON

TABLE 2

"BRISTOL—GREYHOUND"

EACH COLUMN READS :— SINGLE, DAY RETURN, PERIOD RETURN

BASIC FARES

To apply Daily throughout the year, excluding Friday Nights and Saturdays from 22nd May to 26th September.

WESTON-SUPER-MARE			Wells			Shepton Mallet			Frome			Trowbridge			Bradford-on-Avon			Melksham			Devizes			Beckhampton			
–	–	–																									Wells
8/–	9/–	11/–	–	–	–																						Shepton Mallet
8/–	9/–	12/–	–	–	–	–	–	–																			Frome
8/–	9/–	12/–	5/–	5/–	7/–	4/–	5/–	7/–	–	–	–																Trowbridge
9/–	9/–	13/–	5/–	6/–	8/–	5/–	5/–	7/–	–	–	–	–	–	–													Bradford-on-Avon
10/–	12/–	17/–	7/–	8/–	12/–	6/–	7/–	9/–	4/–	5/–	6/–	–	–	–	–	–	–										Melksham
11/–	12/–	18/–	7/–	9/–	13/–	7/–	8/–	12/–	4/–	5/–	8/–	4/–	–	6/–	–	–	–	–	–	–							Devizes
11/–	12/–	20/–	8/–	11/–	14/–	8/–	9/–	13/–	6/–	6/–	10/–	5/–	6/–	8/–	5/–	5/–	7/–	4/–	5/–	7/–	–	–	–				Beckhampton
12/–	13/–	21/–	11/–	13/–	18/–	11/–	12/–	17/–	7/–	8/–	13/–	6/–	7/–	9/–	6/–	7/–	9/–	5/–	5/–	8/–	5/–	5/–	7/–	–	–	–	Marlborough
13/–	15/–	24/–	13/–	13/–	21/–	12/–	13/–	18/–	9/–	11/–	14/–	8/–	9/–	13/–	7/–	9/–	13/–	6/–	8/–	11/–	5/–	7/–	8/–	–	–	–	SWINDON
14/–	16/–	25/–	13/–	14/–	22/–	13/–	13/–	20/–	10/–	12/–	17/–	9/–	11/–	15/–	8/–	9/–	14/–	7/–	8/–	11/–	6/–	7/–	9/–	5/–	6/–	8/–	Shrivenham
14/–	17/–	26/–	13/–	14/–	22/–	13/–	14/–	20/–	11/–	12/–	17/–	9/–	11/–	17/–	9/–	11/–	16/–	8/–	9/–	13/–	7/–	8/–	12/–	6/–	7/–	9/–	Faringdon
16/–	19/–	28/–	14/–	16/–	24/–	13/–	15/–	21/–	12/–	14/–	18/–	11/–	12/–	17/–	10/–	12/–	17/–	9/–	11/–	14/–	8/–	9/–	14/–	7/–	8/–	11/–	Kingston Bagpuize
16/–	20/–	28/–	14/–	16/–	24/–	14/–	16/–	22/–	13/–	14/–	20/–	12/–	13/–	18/–	11/–	13/–	17/–	10/–	12/–	17/–	9/–	11/–	14/–	8/–	9/–	13/–	Abingdon
17/–	20/–	28/–	15/–	18/–	24/–	14/–	16/–	23/–	13/–	15/–	20/–	13/–	14/–	20/–	13/–	13/–	20/–	12/–	13/–	17/–	10/–	12/–	17/–	9/–	9/–	14/–	OXFORD
17/–	21/–	28/–	16/–	19/–	26/–	15/–	18/–	25/–	14/–	16/–	24/–	14/–	14/–	21/–	13/–	14/–	20/–	13/–	13/–	18/–	12/–	12/–	17/–	9/–	12/–	16/–	Wheatley
17/–	21/–	28/–	17/–	19/–	27/–	17/–	19/–	25/–	15/–	17/–	24/–	14/–	15/–	22/–	14/–	15/–	21/–	13/–	14/–	20/–	12/–	13/–	18/–	11/–	12/–	17/–	Tetsworth
19/–	21/–	29/–	18/–	20/–	29/–	17/–	20/–	27/–	17/–	18/–	25/–	16/–	16/–	24/–	14/–	16/–	22/–	13/–	15/–	21/–	13/–	14/–	20/–	12/–	13/–	17/–	Stokenchurch
20/–	25/–	36/–	20/–	22/–	33/–	19/–	21/–	30/–	17/–	19/–	26/–	17/–	18/–	25/–	16/–	18/–	24/–	15/–	16/–	23/–	14/–	15/–	22/–	13/–	14/–	20/–	High Wycombe
21/–	27/–	36/–	20/–	23/–	35/–	20/–	22/–	34/–	17/–	20/–	26/–	17/–	19/–	26/–	17/–	18/–	25/–	16/–	18/–	24/–	15/–	16/–	23/–	13/–	15/–	20/–	Beaconsfield
22/–	27/–	39/–	22/–	25/–	37/–	22/–	23/–	36/–	18/–	21/–	30/–	17/–	20/–	29/–	17/–	19/–	27/–	17/–	19/–	26/–	15/–	17/–	24/–	14/–	16/–	22/–	Uxbridge
23/–	27/–	41/–	22/–	26/–	39/–	22/–	25/–	37/–	18/–	23/–	33/–	17/–	21/–	30/–	17/–	20/–	29/–	17/–	19/–	28/–	15/–	19/–	26/–	16/–	18/–	24/–	Ealing
23/–	27/–	41/–	22/–	26/–	39/–	22/–	26/–	37/–	18/–	23/–	33/–	17/–	21/–	30/–	17/–	20/–	29/–	17/–	19/–	28/–	15/–	19/–	26/–	–	–	–	LONDON
13/–	14/–	24/–	12/–	13/–	20/–	12/–	12/–	19/–	8/–	9/–	14/–	7/–	8/–	13/–	7/–	8/–	12/–	6/–	6/–	11/–	5/–	6/–	9/–	4/–	5/–	7/–	Hungerford
15/–	16/–	25/–	13/–	14/–	23/–	13/–	13/–	21/–	9/–	12/–	16/–	8/–	9/–	14/–	8/–	9/–	14/–	7/–	8/–	13/–	7/–	8/–	11/–	4/–	5/–	7/–	Newbury
15/–	16/–	26/–	14/–	15/–	23/–	13/–	14/–	22/–	11/–	12/–	18/–	9/–	9/–	16/–	9/–	9/–	15/–	8/–	8/–	13/–	7/–	8/–	12/–	5/–	5/–	8/–	Thatcham
17/–	19/–	30/–	17/–	17/–	28/–	15/–	16/–	26/–	13/–	14/–	22/–	12/–	13/–	20/–	12/–	13/–	20/–	10/–	12/–	17/–	9/–	11/–	15/–	8/–	8/–	12/–	READING
19/–	20/–	34/–	17/–	20/–	30/–	17/–	19/–	29/–	14/–	16/–	26/–	14/–	15/–	22/–	13/–	15/–	22/–	13/–	13/–	20/–	11/–	13/–	18/–	9/–	11/–	14/–	Maidenhead
20/–	22/–	35/–	18/–	20/–	33/–	18/–	19/–	30/–	16/–	18/–	28/–	14/–	16/–	24/–	14/–	16/–	24/–	13/–	14/–	22/–	13/–	14/–	20/–	11/–	12/–	17/–	Slough
20/–	23/–	36/–	19/–	20/–	33/–	18/–	20/–	31/–	17/–	18/–	29/–	15/–	16/–	24/–	15/–	16/–	24/–	14/–	14/–	22/–	13/–	14/–	21/–	12/–	12/–	17/–	Colnbrook
23/–	27/–	41/–	22/–	26/–	39/–	22/–	26/–	37/–	18/–	23/–	33/–	17/–	21/–	30/–	17/–	20/–	29/–	17/–	19/–	28/–	15/–	19/–	26/–	14/–	16/–	22/–	LONDON

Marlborough			SWINDON or Chiseldon			Shrivenham			Faringdon			Kingston Bagpuize			Abingdon			OXFORD			Wheatley			
–	–	–																						SWINDON or Chiseldon
5/–	5/–	7/–	–	–	–																			Shrivenham
5/–	5/–	8/–	–	–	–	–	–	–																Faringdon
6/–	8/–	9/–	–	–	–	–	–	–	–	–	–													Kingston Bagpuize
7/–	8/–	11/–	6/–	–	9/–	6/–	–	9/–	–	–	–	–	–	–										Abingdon
8/–	9/–	12/–	6/–	–	10/–	6/–	–	9/–	–	–	–	–	–	–	–	–	–							OXFORD
8/–	9/–	14/–	6/–	9/–	10/–	6/–	8/–	9/–	6/–	8/–	9/–	–	–	–	–	–	–	–	–	–				Wheatley
9/–	11/–	14/–	7/–	9/–	11/–	6/–	8/–	11/–	6/–	8/–	10/–	–	–	–	–	–	–	–	–	–	–	–	–	Tetsworth
9/–	12/–	16/–	8/–	9/–	13/–	7/–	9/–	11/–	7/–	9/–	10/–	7/–	9/–	10/–	7/–	9/–	10/–	7/–	–	10/–	7/–	–	10/–	Stokenchurch
12/–	13/–	18/–	9/–	12/–	14/–	8/–	9/–	13/–	8/–	9/–	12/–	7/–	9/–	10/–	7/–	9/–	10/–	7/–	–	10/–	7/–	–	10/–	High Wycombe
12/–	14/–	20/–	10/–	12/–	17/–	9/–	11/–	14/–	8/–	11/–	14/–	8/–	13/–	14/–	8/–	13/–	14/–	8/–	13/–	14/–	7/–	–	12/–	Beaconsfield
13/–	15/–	20/–	12/–	13/–	19/–	11/–	13/–	19/–	10/–	12/–	16/–	9/–	13/–	16/–	9/–	13/–	15/–	9/–	13/–	15/–	8/–	12/–	14/–	Uxbridge
16/–	16/–	24/–	14/–	16/–	24/–	14/–	16/–	22/–	13/–	13/–	20/–	11/–	13/–	19/–	11/–	13/–	19/–	11/–	13/–	19/–	10/–	12/–	17/–	Ealing
–	–	–	16/–	18/–	24/–	15/–	17/–	23/–	13/–	13/–	20/–	13/–	13/–	20/–	12/–	13/–	19/–	11/–	13/–	19/–	10/–	12/–	17/–	LONDON

10

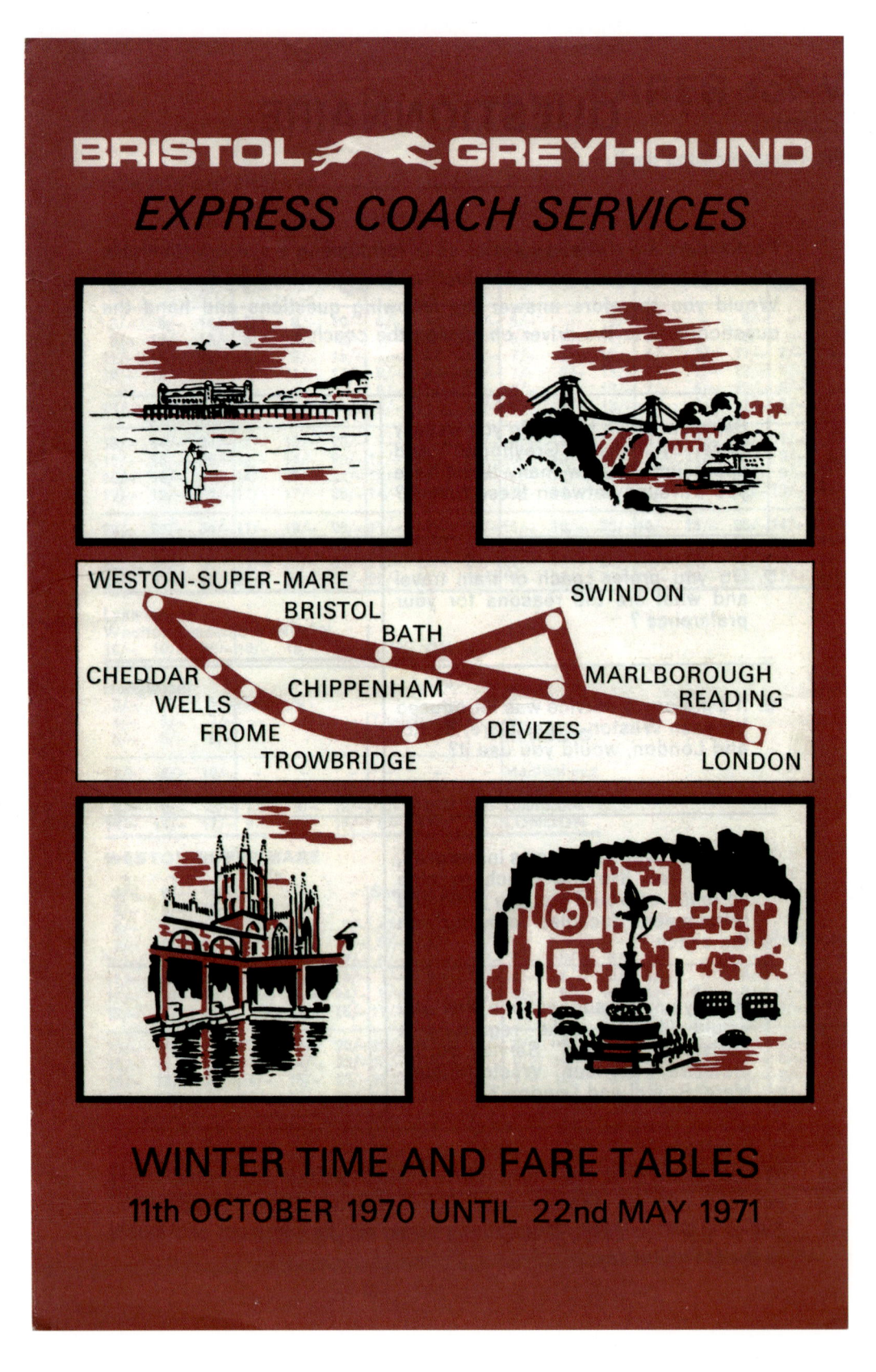

The winter 1970 timetable adopted the new magenta colour scheme and latest, and last, design of Greyhound logo.

APPENDIX 10

EXTRACTS FROM BRISTOL WATCH COMMITTEE RECORD BOOKS, HELD AT BRISTOL RECORD OFFICE. EXTRACTS MADE FROM VOLUME 1, 6TH OCTOBER 1920 UNTIL 31ST DECEMBER 1924, AND VOLUME 2, JANUARY 1925 TO DECEMBER 1930.

It should be noted that the following information related to the correspondence and recommendations of the Watch Committee to their sub-committee and is of its nature one sided information.

8/20 *West Bristol Engineering Works licence application granted for a motor bus service from New Passage to Westbury on Trym*

11/20 *Mr E.A.Oaten applied for a hackney carriage driver's licence. As he had previously been to prison, he was refused. However, in March 1921, he was given a licence.*

27/4/21 *Dolphin motor Co., 327-329 Staple Hill Road, granted a licence for one charabanc. Ashton Gate Motor Co., a 23-seat charabanc with single pneumatic tyres, licence granted.*

8/22 *Complaints were received from the residents of Kennington Road and Gloucester Road that there were too many buses using their suburban roads. After much discussion it was decided to grant no more licences for the time being.*

Petitions from St.Annes Park residents for Mr. Russett to ply for hire between the City and St. Annes. The Watch Committee resolved that they cannot accede to the application.

9/22 *Charles Russett requested to licence a new omnibus to replace an unroadworthy omnibus. Mr E.Jones requested a licence for his charabanc.*
The Committee refused both applications.

8/10/22 *Mr.Jones re-applied for a 14-seat charabanc: licence application deferred. Appealed to Ministry of Transport.*

Regular service buses licenced at that date:

BUSES:

Bristol Tramways	*City routes*	*60*
	Country routes	*39*
	spares and others	*51*
	TOTAL	*150*
Greyhound	*City routes*	*15*
	Spare	*1*
	TOTAL	*16*
Charles Russett	*City routes*	*3*
	Bristol to Keynsham	*1*
	Spare	*1*
	TOTAL	*5*

CHARABANCS

Bristol Tramways	*52*
Greyhound	*13*
Charles Russett	*4*
Others	*75*
TOTAL	*144*

2/4/22 New route Old Market to Robertson Road would now need a new stand at Robertson Road. New stand granted for one class "A" omnibus at Robertson Road, stopping time limited to twenty minutes.

Definition of class "A": Omnibus class "A" means an omnibus that takes up and sets down passengers along its route within the district and in respect of which fares are fixed according to stages with a fare from starting point within the district for the first stage not exceeding nine pence.

The Watch Committee gave approval to the above on 16/5/22.

16/5/22 Greyhound application for route:Colston Street to the junction of Cairns Road and Kellaway Avenue via Jamaica Street, Stokes Croft, Arley Hill, Redland Road and Coldharbour Road. Application acceded to one omnibus, to stand at the junction of Cairns Road and Kellaway Avenue.

Greyhound application to extend the Horfield to Colston Avenue service to Joint Station: application not acceded to.

Bristol Tramways and Carriage Company applied to re-introduce the Old Market to Ashley Down service, which had been curtailed in 1915. Acceded to

16/5/22 W.J.Bence, Bitton-Oldand-Old Market, licence granted, but restricted to the use of one vehicle only.

13/6/22 M.S.Hudson, 19, Daisy Street, Eastville, applied to run from Cassell Road, Fishponds, to Careys Lane or Tramways centre. Application not acceded to.

G.H.Upton, Somerset Garage, Somerset St., Cotham (actually Kingsdown), to run a motor bus from the joint Station to White Tree via Victoria Street, Temple Street, Tower Hill, Careys Lane, Stratton Street, Portland Square, Ashley Road, Cheltenham Road, Cotham Grove, Redland Court Road, Redland Green and Redland Road. The route was not considered a desirable one by the Sub Committee and not acceded to.

Bristol Tramways and Carriage Company route application: Colston Street to Ashley Down via Colston Street, Cheltenham Road, North Road, Cromwell Road, Chesterfield Road, Ashley Hill and Ashley Down Road to the junction of Gloucester Road. Application granted.

15/7/22 Agreed that four standing passengers be allowed on omnibuses: no decision was made concerning trams.

29/3/22 The following stands were recommended for various services as below:

Horsefair	Gloucester, Berkeley, Frampton Cotterell, Chipping Sodbury and Thornbury
Careys Lane	Marshfield
Deanery Road	Bridgwater, Weston super Mare, Clevedon
Telephone Avenue	Clifton, Avonmouth

26/4/22 Recommended that stands in Telephone Avenue to be altered to the east side of the road only, vehicles to face south.
Gloucester Road, St.Phillips stand for 17 omnibuses reduced to 10 at any one time.
Colston Street stand to be increased to 5 from 4 omnibuses.

16/5/22 Bristol Tramways and Carriage Company to operate from the Tramways Centre to Ashley Down via Stokes Croft, Cheltenham Road, Cromwell Road and Chesterfield Road. Not granted at the time but granted on 13/6/22.

9/12/22 Licences granted for regular service omnibuses as follows:

Bristol Tramways	47 City	39 country	9 spares	total 95
Greyhound	12 City	2 spares		total 14
Charles Russett	3 City	1 country	1 spare	total 5

Licences issued for 3 months terminating March 31st 1923.

Buff Motor Co. requested one additional 11 seat charabanc.

21/11/22 Country bus fares to protect local tram services by being higher that the tram fare to places served by trams.
Bristol Tramways and Carriage Company applied for a Bedminster Bridge to Brislington route via Cattle Market Road – decision deferred.

7/12/22 The Chief Constable may authorize the use of extra vehicles for special events, i.e.football matches etc.

The deferred decision on the two route applications by Bristol Tramways and Carriage Company of 21/11/22 were refused.

23/12/22 Bristol Tramways and Carriage Company refused to adhere to the Chief Constables's proposals and had therefore appealed to the Ministry of Transport against the Committee's refusal to grant omnibus licences and their conditions .All proposed licences as at 9/12/22 would be granted for three months.

25/1/23 Charabancs (i.e. not "A" class omnibuses), are not to be used on regular bus services

7/3/23 Sneyd Park omnibus route to stand at Rockleaze as at present.

Operators to fit ticket collection boxes to all class "A" omnibuses.

20/3/23 Charabancs to be removed from Colston Avenue and relocated to Queen Square or Anchor Road. Charabanc proprietors object.

The by-laws to be revised: (1) ninepence to be substituted for sixpence (11) 3 instead of 2 "A" buses.

Stand number 1 (Anchor Road)- Chief Constable to decide which side of Anchor Road charabancs may stand.

New scheme for omnibuses to be introduced 9/4/22.

23/4/23 Greyhound informed the Committee that it was their intention to terminate the new scheme in so far as fares are concerned, as the new fare scheme was detrimental to their business. The Committee stated that a state of chaos would ensue if this was carried out.

Greyhound stated that it was their intention to ask Bristol Tramways and Carriage Company and Charles Russett to reduce their fares: Bristol Tramways would not agree.

2/5/23 Bristol Tramways objection via the Ministry of Transport. If the company's objections extended to the stand at St.Augustine's for the Clyde Road and Sneyd Park buses, they be offered a stopping place on the east side of the Hippodrome on the inward journey and a similar place on the opposite side of the road (near Denmark Street) on the outward journey. Also, the company be offered a stand for the Suspension Bridge bus stand number 11outside the Sun Building, and if the description of the buses to use stand number 12 does not cover the buses plying to Kellaway Avenue, the description be amended to include that destination.

9/5/23 Bristol Tramways objected to putting the Suspension Bridge bus outside the Sun Building and request that the buses should be on stand number 12 in Colston Street. This proposal was approved.

27/6/23 The Committee was informed that a number of charabanc proprietors have taken offices in Colston Avenue and are not complying with the requirements of recent bylaws by advertising their tours from there. This appeared to be directed at defeating the provisions of the bylaws.

1/8/23 The Chief Constable reports that various omnibus proprietors with offices in Colston Avenue are not complying with the requirements of the bylaw and proposed to take action in all infringements brought to his notice.

16/10/23 Charles Russett was reported to the Watch Committee for charging low fares on the Centre to Brislington route, undercutting the tram fares, and given a warning. Greyhound applied for a route from Colston Avenue to St.Werburghs, which was not granted. Greyhound and Bristol Tramways applied jointly for a route to Portishead.

Residents of Berkeley Road, Fishponds, petitioned the Watch Committee complaining of damage caused by buses and asked that an alternative route be substituted: at a subsequent meeting it was decided that no action would be taken.

2/11/23 *Greyhound applied for Bristol to Sneyd Park, Ashton and Portishead routes. Applications refused. Greyhound and the Bristol Tramways decided at a later meeting to jointly appeal to the Minister of Transport.*

13/12/23 *Greyhound applied for a Bristol to Clevedon service, which was refused, and to use double deckers, which was also refused. Charles Russett applied for a spare omnibus, registration PC9201; the application was granted.*

The Watch Committee stated that they were not in favour of Sunday buses and that operators are to be asked to cut down on Sunday working. Greyhound applied for a Bristol to Clevedon route, which was refused.

30/7/24 *Greyhound had appealed to the Minister of Transport about the disallowance of the Clevedon route.*

Bristol Tramways applied to licence fifteen new omnibuses: if this was allowed, no extra buses would ply in congested areas. 15 licences were issued up to 30/9/24.

Bristol Tramways and Greyhound applied jointly to operate to Portishead, each using 2 buses and providing a 45-minute joint service from Prince Street, the service being doubled on Bank Holidays.

14/8/24 *Greyhound applied to operate Bristol, Prince Street, to Clevedon, using 3 buses and not clashing with any other service: the application was refused.*

21/8/24 *Mr.E.Bevan of Thicket Avenue, Fishponds, applied to operate a 15-20 seat motor omnibus from Fishponds tram terminus to Soundwell Road: on 4/11/24 this was not acceded to.*

4/11/24 *Greyhound applied for two routes, Colston Avenue to Staple Hill and Prince Street to Frome – both were refused.*

Bristol Tramways asked to augment the Bristol to Radstock service on weekends, which was granted so long as the Cumberland Basin swing bridge was used. The terminus for the Bristol to Radstock service was to be transferred from Colston Avenue to Prince Street.

Greyhound applied to augment the Fishponds service. Which was refused.

28/1/25 *Bristol Tramways applied for 5 routes:*

Bristol to Clifton (3 licences)
Eastville to Downs via Horfield (3 licences)
Stapleton to Fishponds
To extend the North View service to Filton
Westbury district services (A) and (B) (2 licences.
All granted.

All new and future omnibuses to be fitted with pneumatic tyres.

T.Croydon applied to operate Centre to Kingswood, which was refused.

The Cumberland Road Bridge to be closed for 12 months from 16/2/25: bus services to use Broad Quay, Prince Street and Prince Street Bridge.

24/2/25 *Greyhound applied for the following routes:*

Colston Avenue-Fishponds-Kingswood	*deemed unsuitable.*
Fishponds to Kingswood	*decision deferred*
Eastville-Westbury on Trym-Coombe Dingle	*decision deferred*
Prince Street-Cossham	*deemed unsuitable*
Colston Avenue-Southmead	*deemed unsuitable*

Pioneer applied for the following routes:
St.Agnes Road-St.Pauls Church-Coronation Road
St.Georges Road-St.Pauls Church-Coronation Road

Horsefair-Thornbury
Careys Lane-Barton Hill-Brislington
All were refused on 24/3/25.

24/3/25 *The Committee were resolved to grant licences for the following routes:*

(1) *Cheltenham Road to Suspension Bridge, Bristol Tramways, 3 licences.*
Route: Cotham Brow (bottom of), Cotham Road, St. Michaels Hill, Tyndalls Park Road, - across Whiteladies Road - , St.Pauls Road, Queens Road, Victoria Square, Merchants Road, Regent Street, Clifton Down Road, Gloucester Road, approach to Suspension Bridge.,

(2) *Eastville to Durdham Downs, Bristol Tramways 2 licences, Greyhound 1 licence.*
Route: Napier Road, Stapleton Road, Dormer Road, Muller Road, Wellington Hill, Kellaway Avenue, Coldharbour Road, Iddisleigh Road, Durdham Park, Durdham Downs (corner of Stoke Road).

(3) *Extensions of Colston Street to North View service to Southmead and Filton, Bristol Tramways 2 licences.*
Route: North View, Westbury Road, Henleaze Road, Southmead Road, Filton Church.

(4) *Westbury on Trym and Coombe Dingle, Bristol Tramways, 2 licences.*
Route: Westbury tram terminus, Stoke Lane, Coombe Dingle, Coombe Lane, Canford Road, Westbury tram terminus.(Licence granted on condition that the service does not start until the road is complete, which is anticipated will be in two weeks time.

(5) *Westbury tram terminus via Henbury Road, Henbury Lane, Brentry, Brentry Hill, Passage Road, and back to Westbury tram terminus.*

Consideration of the application from Greyhound Motors Limited to operate an omnibus service from Fishponds to Kingswood was deferred pending a report from the City Engineers as to making provision for foot passengers crossing the railway bridge in Filwood Road.

<u>The Bristol to London Omnibus Service</u>

The Town Clerk read a letter which he had written to the Ministry of Transport enquiring whether the Ministry had given approval to a scale of fares submitted by Greyhound Motors for intermediate places between Bristol and Bath on the 27th January last, and submitted a reply to the effect that a decision by the Ministry on the appeal was not required as Bath Corporation agreed to re-consider the application made to them by the company who, they understood, had agreed to the suggestion made by the Corporation of Bath that the first fare stage on the west side of Bath should be at Newton St. Loe on the east side at Chippenham, without intermediate fares.

Resolved, that the Watch Committee will be recommended to renew the licence in respect of this service for a further period of one month, subject to a written undertaking being given by the Greyhound Motors Limited to entirely remove the seat in front of the emergency exit with its supports and fittings from the omnibuses engaged on this route, and to their giving a further written undertaking that they will not charge intermediate fares between Bristol and Bath, and that the fare between these two places shall be 1/3d.

<u>Pneumatic Tyres</u>

Resolved: that having regard to the fact that the use of pneumatic tyres on omnibuses caused very much less wear and tear on roads and considerably lessens the amount of vibration and noise (complaints of which have been frequently received during the past two years), this Sub-Committee is of the opinion that the time has come when motor buses plying for hire within the City should be fitted with pneumatic tyres in the place of solid tyres, and they ask for authority and approval of the Watch Committee to their taking such steps as may be considered desirable to endeavor to introduce the change.

An application was submitted from Messrs. Bence and Son of Longwell Green for licences in respect of four charabancs to ply for hire in Bristol. Resolved, to accede to this request for six months.

A letter was received from the secretary of the Hillfields Park Estate Tenants association complaining of the inconvenience caused by the frequent breaking down of the "Pioneer" omnibuses serving the route. Resolved: the attention of the proprietor be drawn to the complaint and that he be informed that, unless these omnibuses are put into and maintained in a satisfactory condition, the Committee will seriously consider the advisability of refusing to renew the existing licences in respect thereof. Signed, C.Robinson, Chairman, 19/5/25

19/5/25 *the Town Clerk submitted a letter from the Minister of Transport stating that the Minister would not be prepared to support a condition on an omnibus licence requiring the use of pneumatic tyres as, in his opinion, such tyres are not essential for use on omnibuses.*

A letter from Greyhound Motors Limited, referring to their recent application to inaugurate an omnibus service between Fishponds and Kingswood, and asking that they should be allowed to temporarily run their buses to Fishponds via Lodge Causeway or as an alternative to stop at the Kingswood end of Filwood Road railway bridge. Resolved: Request acceded to pending the widening of the bridge. The Chief Constable was authorized to determine the number of licences required.

Greyhound Motors applied to operate between Hotwells and Westbury tram terminus via Bridge Valley Road. Resolved: That the route was sufficiently served over the major portion of the route, and that the remainder of the route was unfit for omnibuses.

Greyhound Motors applied for permission to extend the Sneyd Park and Ashton service to either Long Ashton Cider Institute or the Cross Hands at Bedminster Down. Resolved: To approve the extension of the service to Bedminster Down and to offer the same concession to Bristol Tramways.

A further application received from Greyhound Motors to extend the Centre to Fishponds (Cassell Road) service to Mangotsfield. Resolved: No action can be taken as the whole of the proposed extension is outside of the City.

Greyhound Motors submitted a letter asking the Committee to take steps to prevent Bristol Tramways from using the authorized stand outside the premises of Greyhound at St.Augustines Parade, which, they alleged, interfered with the conduct of their business. Resolved: That Greyhound be informed that the Sub Committee cannot see their way to interfere in the matter, having regard to all of the circumstances.

An application was also made by Greyhound Motors to increase the Eastville to Downs service during the forthcoming Whitsuntide. Resolved: To accede to the request subject to all other services being maintained in the normal way.

12/8/25 *It was also resolved that notice be given to each of the omnibus proprietors stating that any future meetings of the Watch Committee(Traffic Sub Committee) will be held at the beginning of March, June, September and December in each year and that any application for consideration by the Sub Committee to the Town Clerk must be submitted not later than the first of each of the above mentioned months.*

An application was received from Greyhound Motors to extend the Fishponds to Durdham Downs service via The Promenade to the Suspension Bridge, giving a 15-minutes service. Resolved: To grant the application.

An application was received from Greyhound Motors to run over Lodge Causeway Bridge: Resolved: To defer the decision until December next.

17/8/25 *Resolved: To recommend to the Watch Committee as follows:*

Bristol Tramways Applications	Recommendations
Colston Street to Avonmouth	3 additional licences
Clyde Road to Bedminster	1 additional licence
Prince Street to Bishopsworth	1 additional licence
Prince Street to Luckwell Road	not granted, route unsuitable
Knowle, Whitchurch, Keynsham and Brislington	1 new licence
Careys Lane to Cossham	not granted, route unsuitable

Careys Lane to Stapleton	*2 new licences*
Fishponds to Frenchay and Hambrook	*1 new licence*
Careys Lane and Greenbank	*not granted, route unsuitable*
Greyhound Motors Applications	*Recommendations*
Durdham Downs to Sea Mills	*not granted, route un-necessary*
Durdham Downs to Blaise Castle the entrance to the grounds	*deferred: existing route operates past*
Careys Lane to Ashley Down extension	*1 licence to Greyhound*
	1 licence to Bristol Tramways (if Bristol Tramways did not wish to participate then both licences would go to Greyhound)
Centre, Eastville, Hillfields Park and Fishponds	*not granted*
Centre to Sion Hill (Rocks Railway)	*not granted*
Horsefair to Sion Hill (Rocks Railway)	*not granted*

17/12/25 *Resolved: To recommend to the Watch Committee as follows:*

Greyhound Motors applications	*Recommendations*
Centre to Sion Hill (Rocks Railway)	*neither granted, suggested alternative*
Horsefair to Sion Hill (Rocks Railway)	*routes via Lower Clifton Hill unsuitable*
Augmentation of Sneyd Park to Bedminster Down service	*not granted, not required at present*
Prince Street to Dundry	*2 new licences granted*
Prince Street and London	*1 new licence granted*

An application by Greyhound to employ two double deck omnibuses on the Colston Avenue and Fishponds route in substitution of two single deck licences, subject to the double deckers being new and of the same type as the existing double deck omnibuses, was granted.

3/2/26 Licencing of Double Deck omnibuses

The Sub Committee considered an application from Greyhound Motors Limited for a licence for a covered top omnibus to ply for hire on the Tramways Centre to Fishponds route. The chairman has stated that the Committee had inspected the vehicle and that the Greyhound Company had undertaken to carry out certain alterations to the vehicle to meet the requirements of the Sub-Committee. It was resolved to allow the vehicle to be licenced in substitution of another vehicle until March 31st next.

Greyhound Motors asked to substitute double deckers for single deckers on the Sneyd Park to Bedminster route, but the Sub-Committee said that the route was unsuitable due to steep hills, although it would not raise any objections to double deckers being used on the Eastville to Downs via Muller Road route. Resolved: To recommend to Bristol Tramways and Greyhound Motors that no objection would be raised to doubling the Portishead service on Saturday afternoons and Sundays if required, and additional licences will be granted for that purpose.

Greyhound Motors applied to operate the London service during the winter months without a conductor. Resolved: To decline the request on safety grounds, and as it would create a precident which was undesirable.

A petition was received from residents of Sion Hill, Clifton, that the omnibus service should be suspended as un-necessary. Resolved: To suspend this service in the winter months, and only to run from April to October inclusive.

29/3/26 *Resolved: To recommend to the Watch Committee as follows:*

Bristol Tramways applications	*Recommendations*
Prince Street to Luckwell Road	*not granted*

Careys Lane to Cossham	not granted
Careys Lane to Stapleton	not granted
Careys Lane to Greenbank	not granted
Fishponds, Causeway, to Wood Road	not granted
Colston Avenue to Filton	acceded to if the route is via Howard Road and Henley Grove, Henleaze
Eastville, Downs to Sion Hill	acceded to if journeys do not use Sion Hill and terminate at the Clifton Rocks Hotel

Greyhound Motors applications

Knowle Park to Prince Street	not granted
Prince Street to St. George	not granted
Careys Lane to Westbury Park	not granted
Horsefair to Zoo	not granted
Eastville, Downs to Sion Hill	granted as Bristol Tramways above
Colston Avenue to Southmead Road	additional rush hour buses granted
Sneyd Park to Bedminster	not granted
Downs to Blaise Castle	2 licences granted in summer, plus 1 licence to Bristol Tramways, but deferred until the woods were opened to the public

Mr C Russett applications

Careys Lane, Barton Hill to Brislington	not granted
Careys Lane or Colston Avenue to Soundwell Road	not granted
St. Georges Park to Ashton Avenue	not granted
Prince Street to Avonmouth	not granted

Licences would not be acceded to unless new omnibuses be substituted for the existing fleet.

17/6/26 Resolved: To recommend to the Watch Committee as follows:

Greyhound Motors applications	Recommendations
Sneyd Park to Bedminster Down: application to discontinue the portion of this route between Ashton Avenue and Bedminster Down	granted if no augmentation of the remainder of the route is allowed and the vehicle allocation reverts to the position before the extension was licenced
Prince Street to Portishead	matter left with the Chief Constable. Granted during August Bank Holiday but this permission is not to be taken as a general augmentation of this service
Centre to Zoo	as above
Eastville to Downs and Suspension Bridge	permission granted to all companies to augment this service during August Bank Holiday (31st July to 4th August)

The existing services granted to Bristol Tramways, Greyhound Motors and Pioneer in respect of regular omnibus
Services be granted for a further three months.

<u>Covered double deck omnibuses</u>
Permission granted for use on Colston Avenue to Fishponds route, subject to such vehicles being new and of an approved type. The Sub Committee also acceded to said double deckers being used on the Eastville, Downs and Suspension Bridge service.

The Portway
Subject to arrangements as to "through fares" on tramways and buses of both companies, eight licences will be granted, six to Bristol Tramways and two to Greyhound Motors, subject to the following conditions:

- *City terminus will be the site of the old Port Railway and Pier Station*
- *All omnibuses have pneumatic tyres*
- *Headlights to be dimmed and windows on the nearside of buses to be screened at night-times (offside on return journey).*
- *Double deck buses can be used but no trailers are permitted*
- *Signs are to be erected at both ends of the Portway for all motorcars to dim their lights*

Route applications: Recommendations:

Bristol Tramways

Route	Recommendation
Prince Street to Luckwell Road	refused
Careys Lane to Cossham	refused
Careys Lane to Stapleton	refused
Careys Lane to Greenbank	refused
Clyde Road to Bedminster (augmentation)	refused
Colston Street to Suspension Bridge (augmentation)	refused
Durdham Downs to Sea Walls	refused
Fishponds, Causeway, to Wood Road Lodge Causeway Bridge	deferred pending completion of
Westbury to Blaise Castle	1 licence granted
Durdham Downs to Coombe Dingle	deferred

Greyhound Motors

Route	Recommendation
Bristol and Blaise Castle	refused

The Sub Committee decided to recommend that in future all applications for new omnibus services should, (special cases excepted), be considered annually, but the practice now obtaining, of renewing existing licences every three months, be continued

23/6/26 *The modification to the Ashton to Sneyd Park service by Greyhound Motors Limited be granted, but that Bristol Tramways wished to continue its part as existing, and this was granted.*

With regard to the Portway route, Bristol Tramways would not allow "through fares" to be issued by Greyhound buses and also Greyhound took exception to only being allowed 2 licences whilst Bristol Tramways were granted six. Also, although both companies agreed to use buses with pneumatic tyres, they were not prepared to give such undertaking in writing. The matter concerning "through fares" be referred to the Watch committee" for their decision.

6/7/26 *Mr Charles Russett had asked for permission to come before the Sub-Committee to place his views with regard to the refusal by the Watch Committee to grant additional licences. The Sub-Committee then interviewed Mr. Russett, who stated that he had made numerous applications for additional omnibus licences and in each case his applications had been refused. He alleged that the statements made, that his buses were constantly breaking down and in an unfit condition for public use were entirely unfounded and he asked that additional licences should be granted to him in respect of the route via Avondale Road to Ashton and additional licences to ply for hire on the Brislington and Fishponds routes.*

In reply the Chairman stated that complaints had been received from time to time, both from the public and the police, with regard to the condition of these buses and that if he wished the Committee to consider any application he must maintain his buses in a proper condition and see that the timetables were strictly complied with. If Mr. Russett submitted his applications in writing at the proper time, they would be considered when the Committee were next meeting for the purpose of considering new applications.

The Portway

The Chief Constable reported that Bristol Tramways and Greyhound Motors had started their Portway service between Hotwells and Avonmouth. The attention of the Sub-Committee was drawn to the necessity of finding a suitable turning point for the buses at the Hotwells end of the Portway, and of the danger of traffic turning from Bridge Valley Road onto the Portway, and vice-versa. The Chief Constable was requested to report on the matter.

Application by Gough's Motor Garage to operate Temple Meads to Avonmouth, via the Portway	Refused, on the grounds that existing services were adequate

Bristol to London

Greyhound applied to augment this service during the Summer	2 additional licences granted subject to pneumatic tyres being fitted and vehicles are of a satisfactory Type and condition.

Bedminster Down to Dundry via Kings Head Lane route

The Town Clerk informed the Sub-Committee that the Watch Committee referred them to a letter from the Bedminster Down tenants association asking that representation should be made to the Tramways Company for a revision of the existing fare stages on the above route. The Sub-Committee cannot interfere as the major part of this route is outside of the City, but their letter would be passed on to the Bristol Tramways Company.

Residents of Henley Grove complained of the danger caused by omnibuses using that road, by reason of the narrowness of the road and the nature of the corner of Henley Grove and Henleaze Road. It was resolved that the Bristol Tramways Company be asked to revert to the previous route used, via Henleaze Avenue.

27/7/26   Birmingham and Midland Motor Omnibus Company applied to ply for hire whilst passing through Bristol on their Weston super Mare service. It was resolved to allow this application if only one bus is used at a time, and to confine their buses to the route at present operated by their buses.

Sir John Swaish (Chairman of the Watch Committee) submitted a letter which he had received from residents of Clifton calling attention to the damage caused by buses stopping at corners. It was resolved to refer their letter to the Chief Constable

1/9/26   *Bristol to London service*

The Chief Constable reported that Greyhound Motors had two licences granted from 19/11/24: this was doubled to four from 1/4/26, and increased to six from 6/7/26, and an application had now been received to increase this to ten licences. It was resolved to grant these licences subject to the usual conditions.

Plying for hire from garage to place of service

It had been reported that persons had assembled in the morning at the starting point of a service, only to find that the omnibus was full, having picked up at the garage and en-route prior to taking up service. It was resolved that proprietors be informed that this practice must cease forthwith.

Omnibuses at Sneyd Park

The Chief Constable reported that there were four omnibuses employed on the Sneyd Park and Bedminster Down route giving a 15-minute service, and that until recently the terminus of the service at Sneyd Park was at the junction of Ivywell Road with The Avenue, which required the omnibuses reversing to get into position for the return journey, and also entails their standing inside the traffic lines whilst waiting. In consequence, the starting place was moved about thirty yards from the junction to a position outside "The Heath", the occupier of which strongly complained of the annoyance caused by omnibuses standing outside of his house, and since the 4th of August the omnibuses have stood at the junction of The Avenue with Julian Road, alongside the boundary hedge of "The Hythe", occupied by Alderman Stroud, who strongly objects to the arrangements on the grounds that it depreciates his property, is a dangerous obstruction to vehicles entering and leaving *his residence, is a nuisance, and is unsuitable for picking up passengers It was resolved that, after very careful consideration, the present arrangements be continued, as this is the minimum of obstruction to traffic and obviates the need to shunt vehicles to turn.*

<u>Beachley to Aust Ferry service</u>

Greyhound Motors Limited had been asked by the ferry company to point out that the absence of a bus service between the ferry and Aust caused considerable inconvenience. The Sub-Committee instructed the Chief Constable to interview Bristol Tramways with a view to extending their service.

14/10/26 *The Chief Constable reported that a request had been received from Alderman Stroud asking that the omnibus terminus of the Sneyd Park route be moved. He also reported that a petition contacting four hundred signatures had been received, together with a number of letters, asking that the terminus should remain as already fixed, as in the opinion of the petitioners the position selected by the Committee was the most convenient to meet the needs of the public. It was resolved that no good ground had been put forward to justify the alteration of the bus terminus at Julian Road.*

Proprietors had agreed not to pick up passengers between the garage to take up points. Greyhound Motors, however, asked to be exempt in respect of their London service coaches and this was acceded to.

21/1/27 *Greyhound Motors applied to use vehicles with galley and toilet facilities on the London service. 2 licences were granted subject to the Chief Constable's approval of suitable arrangements for emptying the lavatory.*

Greyhound Motors requested that as Bristol Tramways and Bath Tramways Motor Company had reduced their fares between Bristol and Bath to one shilling, that their own fares between these two points be adjusted from one shilling and threepence to one shilling. This was approved.

Greyhound Motors asked to augment the Ashton to Sneyd Park route when Bristol City A.F.C are at home. This was granted subject to Bristol Tramways being allowed to do the same.

Greyhound Motors and Bristol Tramways applied to augment the Eastville to Downs service on Saturday afternoons and Sundays. This was granted.

10/3/27 *Class A omnibus licences be granted for 3 months as follows:*

Fishponds Causeway and Hanham

Fishponds and Kingswood, 2 licences to Bristol Tramways and 2 to Greyhound, to be effective on completion of Lodge Causeway bridge and of a suitable terminus in the vicinity of Robertson Road.

Eastville, Downs and Suspension Bridge, from May 1st until September 30th only, Bristol Tramways 4 extra licences, Greyhound 2 extra licences in respect of the extended route.

Colston Avenue, Chipping Sodbury, Malmesbury and Tetbury, Bristol Tramways 2 additional licences.

Horsefair and Suspension Bridge, Greyhound Motors 2 additional licences.

Colston Avenue to Avonmouth via Parrys Lane, Bristol Tramways 2 additional licences

Downs, Coombe Dingle and Westbury, Bristol Tramways 2 additional licences.

Colston Avenue to Ashley Down Road via Cromwell Road, Bristol Tramways 1 additional licence at rush hours.

Cheltenham Road (Kingsley Road) and Suspension Bridge, Bristol Tramways 1 additional licence.

Westbury, New Passage and Severn Beach, Bristol Tramways 1 additional licence.

Colston Avenue to Clevedon and Weston, Bristol Tramways to augment the services on Saturdays and Sundays from May to September, the route to commence from Broad Quay.

Colston Avenue to Radstock via Keynsham, Bristol Tramways 2 additional licences.

Bristol to Bath, Bristol Tramways 2 additional licences.

Bristol to Bournemouth, Greyhound Motors granted 4 licences subject to starting point and fares being approved by the Chief Constable.

Bristol to Birmingham, Greyhound Motors granted 4 licences subject to the starting point and fares being approved by the Chief Constable.

Bristol, Prince Street, and Weymouth, Pioneer granted 2 licences, conditions as above.

Colston Avenue to St.Phillips Marsh, granted subject to starting point being Prince Street and the route via Commercial Road.

Prince Street to Bishopsworth, Greyhound to operate this route as at present or withdrawn entirely.

Careys Lane to Royate Hill, deferred until completion of Gordon Road and Royate Hill.

Service applications not granted (includes augmentations and deviations): operators or conditions of applications not recorded.

Prince Street and Luckwell Road

Prince Street, Wick Road and Brislington

Careys Lane and Stapleton

St.Annes and Ashton

Careys Lane and Stapleton

Careys Lane and Green Bank

Knowle and Ashton Road

Bristol and Malmesbury

Durdham Downs and Sea Walls

Colston Street and Suspension Bridge

Careys Lane, Eastville and Brislington

Brislington and Eastville

Colston Avenue, Parrys Lane and Avonmouth

Horsefair, Kingsdown and Old Market

Zetland Road and Suspension Bridge

Prince Street and Chew Magna

Fishponds, Hambrook, Stoke Gifford and Filton

Avonmouth and Severn Beach

Horsefair and Stapleton

Colston Avenue, Kingsdown, Redland and Downs

Careys Lane, Ashley Hill and Westbury

Careys Lane, Kingswood and Hanham

Bristol and Thornbury

Deviation of Colston Avenue and Cassell Road service via Channons Hill and Manor Road

Careys Lane, Barton Hill and Brislington

Hotwells and Avonmouth via Portway

St. George and Ashton

Careys Lane or Colston Avenue and Soundwell Road

Careys Lane, St. Phillips Marsh and Colston Avenue

Colston Avenue and Keynsham

16/3/27 *Recommended that:*

Careys Lane to Royate Hill, one additional licence to Greyhound Motors, subject to discontinuance of the service from Eastville Junction to Kingsway/Bryants Hill Road.

Blackboy Hill and Sea Mills, to divert this service via Coombe Dingle, the viaduct, and Sylvan Way.

Colston Street and Avonmouth, 3 additional licences granted for this route provided no increase made in the number of buses standing at Colston Street.

Prince Street and Chew Magna, 2 additional licences but new route via Dundry Hill not to be granted.

Careys Lane and Eastville and Careys Lane and Horfield, additional licences to be granted, 1 to Bristol Tramways and 1 to Greyhound Motors.

Colston Street and Suspension Bridge, two additional licences granted.

Sneyd Park and Bedminster Down: as Greyhound Motors did not augment this service as previously requested, permission should be withdrawn and the application to augment the Victoria Rooms and Ashton Avenue service should not be granted.

Knowle and Cheddar Grove: in consequence of the number of buses using St.Johns Lane, the licences granted to Bristol Tramways and Greyhound Motors to operate this service should be withdrawn.

4/5/27   *The Chairman informed the Sub-Committee that they had been called together for the purpose of receiving a deputation from the St. Phillps Marsh Vigilance and Improvement Committee, asking the Committee to grant a licence to Mr. Charles Russett to operate an omnibus service from the City to meet the requirements of the residents of the St. Phillips Marsh district. The Sub-Committee then interviewed the deputation who pointed out that the existing route operated by Mr. Russett did not meet the requirement of the neighbourhood and that Mr. Russett was prepared to forgo his licence in respect of this route if the Sub-Committee would approve an omnibus service being operated along the following route: Victoria Street Square, Short Street, Feeder Road, Marsh Road, Avon Street, Horton Street, Midland Road, Lawford Street, Redcross Street and Careys Lane, with a detour on the return journey via Old Market., an hourly service being suggested. It was resolved that the Chief Constable be requested to interview Mr. Russett and also inspect the route, and that subject to the Chief Constable being satisfied as to the suitability of the route the necessary licence would be granted.*

Elliot Brothers (Royal Blue) of Bournemouth asked for a licence for operation between Bristol and Bournemouth: it was resolved that as there was sufficient service already, the request was to be refused.

Greyhound Motors asked to augment the Colston Avenue to Strathmore Road service to run every 10 minutes instead of every 15 minutes, 1extra licence being required. It was resolved to grant the licence.

Alderman Stroud submitted a request that the Bedminster and Sneyd Park route be re-routed at the Sneyd Park end. It was resolved that the existing route was satisfactory.

Greyhound Motors asked to augment the Sneyd Park and Bedminster Downs service to every 12 minutes and to incorporate the Colston Avenue to Fishponds (Cassell Road) service with the Eastville, Kingswood and Hanham service. It was resolved that both would be refused.

Charles Russett applied to make the following amendments to his licences:
- *(a) An extra bus on Bristol to Keynsham on Saturdays and Sundays*
- *(b) Augment his Hillfields, Fishponds and Old Market service*
- *(c) To deflect his Centre to Brislington service to certain firms to meet the requirements of the St. Phillips Marsh district.*

It was resolved to accede to this request.

13/10/27 *Stephen Albert Ball submitted an application to run from Bristol to Dundry. He had been proceded against for plying for hire without a licence and undertook, when before the magistrates, to apply for a licence. The Chief Constable reported that Ball was a carrier from Dundry and that the police did not interfere as long as the carriers brought their passengers from Dundry to various Hotel yards, and picked up again from these yards, and that the carriers were now complying with this arrangement.*

Residents of Westbury and Redland asked that the Eastville, Downs and Suspension Bridge service to be continued through the winter for the benefit of schools and Bristol Rugby. It was resolved to grant an extension until December 31st next.

Hillfields Park service between Argyle Hall and Crofts End Road had become dangerous and it is recommended that the route be diverted via Speedwell Road rather than Whitehall Road.

22/11/27 S.A.Ball, omnibus licence applied for to ply for hire between Dundry and Bristol, not granted as carriers provide an adequate service.

Greyhound Motors applied to extend the Old Market to Filton Avenue service to the Duke of York Hotel near Horfield Barracks, pending construction of a new road. Application deferred.

Charles Russett applied for an additional omnibus on their Centre to Keynsham route. Application deferred.

16/3/28 Lack of supervision on the Hillfields Park route means that no new licences will be granted to Mr.Russett until his current vehicles are replaced by new or more satisfactory vehicles.

Carey's lane to Royate Hill, Bristol Tramways to be given one licence, Greyhound to be given one licence, subject to the discontinuance of the Eastville Junction with junctions of Kingsway and Bryants Hill route.

Blackboy Hill and Sea Mills, granted to divert this service via Coombe Dingle, The Viaduct and Sylvan Way.

Colston Street and Avonmouth, 3 extra licences to Bristol Tramways, providing no extra vehicles stand at Colston Street.

Prince Street and Chew Magna via Dundry, Bristol Tramways, 2 extra licences but no licences in respect of the new route via Dundry Hill and Chew Magna.

Carey's Lane and Eastville,	Bristol Tramways and Greyhound one extra licence.
Carey's Lane and Horfield	for each route.
Colston St. and Suspension Bridge	Bristol Tramways 2 extra licences

Carey's Lane & Horfield application of Bristol Tramways and Greyhound to be deferred until the Filton Avenue extension is completed.

Greyhound Motors.

Sneyd Park and Bedminster Down: as the augmentation had not been carried out at rush hours, permission is now withdrawn. Also, augmentation of the Ashton Avenue to Victoria Rooms service not to be granted.

Knowle to Cheddar Grove, Bristol Tramways and Greyhouind licences to be withdrawn due to the number of buses using St Johns Lane.

Knowle Tram Terminus and Greyhound Track, Greyhound refused, Bristol Tramways reduced to 2 licences, but it is requested that the route be suspended (no Greyhound buses to the Greyhound Track!).

Pioneer

Colston Avenue to Keynsham, proposed extension approved but no additional licences to be granted unless his current vehicles are replaced.

Prince St. to Weymouth, the licence granted to Mr. Russett for one vehicle be withdrawn until the service can be fully operated.

Bristol and Bath, Bristol Tramways, that the licences be withdrawn if the Newton St. Loe route is not extended to Bath by 30th June 1928.

Bristol Tramways

Bristol to Burnham, permission withdrawn.

Bristol to Birmingham, permission withdrawn

Upper Belgrave Road. To continue as present.

The following were not granted:

Prince St. to Luckwell Rd.	*Zetland Rd., Horfield, Westbury, Southmead.*
Carey's lane to Cossham.	*Prince Street, St.George, via Feeder Rd. and Fishponds.*
Carey's Lane to Stapleton.	*Bristol – Thornbury.*
Prince St. to Brislington.	*Bedminster – Durdham Down.*
Knowle to Ashton.	*Carey's Lane or Colston St. to Shirehampton.*
Downs to Sea Walls.	*Carey's Lane to Hilfields Park.*
Prince St. to Portishead.	*Carey's Lane, Barton Hill and Brislington.*

It was resolved to recommend to the Watch Committee on granting new licences is that they shall be operated by 30th September next and are granted for 3 month, subject to conditions being complied with and vehicles maintained in a proper mechanical condition otherwise to the satisfaction of the Chief Constable, and that time tables and fares are adhered to and stopping places are observed

Elliot Bros. (Royal Blue), Bournemouth) Ltd., applied for 24 new licences for vehicles to pass through Bristol on their London, Bournemouth and Weston Super Mare services and that not more than two will be used on each route in a day.

Recommended provided no more than four buses are used on each service in Bristol daily and that they are routed via Bath Rd., York Rd., Coronation Rd., Cliff House Rd. and Ashton Avenue, that the required licences be acceded to. In view of a number of serious accidents occurring it suggests that the vehicles should be provided with rear exits.

12/12/28

Greyhound	*Bristol to Coventry approved.* *Bristol to Northampton approved.*
Black & White	*Bristol to Cheltenham approved, provided that minimum fares are observed locally and that vehicles pick up and set down at the Horsefair, and the service starts by 21st February 1929.*
Glider Pullman	*Bristol, Gloucester, Worcester, Birmingham, deferred until a definite proposition is placed before the Committee.*
Holt Bros., Rochdale	*Blackpool and Torquay, approved if route through Bristol is: Southmead Rd., Henleaze Rd., Upper Belgrave Rd., Bridge Valley Rd., Cumberland Basin, Swing Bridge, Ashton Avenue and Winterstoke Rd*

	Minimum fares	*Bristol – Langport*	*1/6d*
		Bristol – Gloucester	*3/-*

Dates are not yet fixed.

D.Clifford, Sutton, Surrey	*To operate an omnibus service between Plymouth and Birmingham. (Approved on the same condition as the Holt service in this district).*
Greyhound	*Coventry to Paignton (10/12/28), asked for additional licences to operate Bristol – Paignton, Bristol – Coventry, via Bath and Stroud, one bus daily between Coventry and Paignton.*
	The Committee had no objections providing the usual local conditions were observed.
	Bristol to Northampton via Bath, Swindon and Oxford, 2 licences for 2 daily journeys required, minimum fare between Bristol and Bath 1/-.
Black & White	*Bristol and Cheltenham, 2 daily services, 6 licences required, not more than 2 to be used at any one time. Fare to and from Gloucester not to be less than 3/-. They wished to operate from Denmark St., but were requested to start from Horsefair.*

16/4/29

Bristol Tramways	*Routes not acceded to:*

Prince St. to Luckwell Rd.   Carey's Lane to Stapleton.
Prince St. to Brislington   Knowle to Ashton.
Broad Plain, Raleigh Rd. to Southville.

Bristol Tramways	*Applied to extend Avonmouth – Hotwells service to Prince St: deferred concerning fares etc.*

Colston St. to Suspension Bridge: in order that buses can approach and depart by alternative routes from Merchants Rd. to obviate the need to reverse on Sion Hill. This was acceded to. Also, vehicles setting down outside the Hippodrome can turn around the triangle to take up passengers at the ferry Steps for the return journey. This was acceded to. It was also requested to extend the service to Temple Meads, but this was not acceded to.

Bristol Tramways	*Requested to extend the Carey's Lane to Horfield service to Temple Meads. Not granted.*
Bristol Tramways	*Colston Avenue to Ashley Down, an additional licence was asked for to extend this service to Temple Meads. Not granted.*

Carey's Lane to Royate Hill, that the operation of that portion of the existing omnibus service between Royate Hill and Carey's Lane on the Carey's Lane to Fishponds service, with the consent of the Companies concerned be discontinued and that the service be terminated at Robertson Rd. Each company to surrender one licence.

Bristol Tramways	*Carey's Lane to Briar way, Fishponds, one extra licence requested. Not acceded to.*
Bristol Tramways	*Westbury to Charlton, to extend the Westbury to Brentry and Henbury service to Charlton. Acceded to.*
Bristol Tramways	*Colston St. to Filton and Avonmouth, 2 extra licences to provide a 15 minute service between Colston St. and the junction of Southmead Rd. and Wellington Hill. Acceded to.*
Bristol Tramways	*Prince St. and Frome, 2 extra licences requested. Acceded to.*
Bristol Tramways	*Prince St. to Wells and Street, 1 extra licence to provide an hourly service. Acceded to.*

4/6/29   *With reference to the applications by Bristol Tramways to extend services to Temple Meads Station, Mr. Vernon Smith and Col. Smith stated in an interview the following points to be taken into consideration:*

(a) *That the public travelling to Temple Meads who desire to use the tramway service would still be served by the Brislington service.*

(b) *That the passengers using the omnibus routes would be enabled to go direct to the station.*

(c) *That congestion at the Tramways Centre would be lessened by the discontinuance of the Tramways Centre to Station service.*

(d) *That if required the proposed new bus service over Bristol Bridge could be worked as a one way system.*

Workers fares: the Committee asked Bristol Tramways to consider whether they could consider introducing workmen's fares on bus routes not covered by tram services. The company refused on the grounds that petrol prices had been rising lately and other costs, which meant that there was no possibility of introducing such concessions at present.

It was requested that to help to alleviate congestion the number of tram stopping places to be reduced. Deferred.

Bristol Tramways Taxi Cabs.	*The Watch Committee was informed that of 72 taxi cabs submitted for inspection for licences 14 were turned down as not being fit and the other 58 were turned down with*

		defects. 3 month licences were to be issued to the 58 cabs when rectified.
	Bristol Tramways	*Applied for an extra licence so that the Bristol to Cheltenham service could be extended to Malvern. Granted.*
	Empress Motor Coaches.	*Bristol to Bath was applied for but the application was refused as the route was already well served.*
	Bristol Tramways	*Applied to extend the Ashley Down to Suspension Bridge service to Temple Meads. Appliaction refused.*
	Merseyside Touring Co together with Greyhound Motors Ltd.	*Applied for 6 licences each for Liverpool to Torquay and Bournemouth services. Granted subject to the usual fare and route requirements.*
	Elliot Bros. (Royal Blue),	*Birmingham to Bristol, Weston Super mare, Taunton, Exeter, Torquay and Plymouth services. Request for 70 licences required so that any of its vehicles could be used on any route. This was acceded to providing that the Metropolitan Police licences that were issued to these vehicles be submitted to the Chief Constable for inspection and that minimum fares of 3/- Bristol to Gloucester and 2/- Bristol to Weston Super mare are charged and that prescribed routes through Bristol are followed.*
	Black & White.	*Requested 10 licences for their Cheltenham, Bristol and Weston Super Mare services to stand at Denmark Street so that passengers can use their agents waiting room at Messrs. Godfrey, St. Augustine Parade. This would be acceded to if coaches pick up and set down at Canon's Marsh near to the premises of Rowe Bros. Ltd. Minimum fares to be charged between Bristol and Gloucester and Bristol and Weston Super Mare.*
	L.W. Andrews,	*A motor coach of unusual design and layout was submitted. One vehicle licence acceded to. (No known unusual vehicle*
6/1/30		
	Bristol Tramways	*Requested to extend Suspension Bridge to Ashley Down services to Temple Meads. Refused.*
	Merseyside Touring Co. Ltd. and Greyhound,	*Daily Liverpool, Torquay and Bournemouth, 6 buses each . Granted provided fares of 3/- between Bristol and Gloucester, 1/- between Bristol and Bath and 1/6d between Bristol and Langford.*
	Elliot Bros.), Royal Blue,	*Birmingham to Plymouth 70 licences requested. Granted if Metropolitan Police licences are inspected by the Chief Constable and fares between Bristol and Gloucester are 3/- and between Bristol and Weston Super Mare set at 2/-.*
	Black & White,	*Request that buses stand at the end of Denmark St. Refused. Buses can stand at nearby Canon's Marsh, fares to be set at 3/- single and 5/- return between Bristol and Gloucester and at 2/- between Bristol and Weston Super Mare.*
29/1/30		*The traffic signals at Whiteladies Rd. are now worn out and will shortly need to be replaced. New signals to cost 265 pounds. Accepted.*
8/5/30	*Bristol Tramways Taxi Cabs,*	*Would be withdrawn 16/5/30. Arrangements will be made to provide a reasonable service at Temple Meads.*
	Omnibus licences,	*To recommend as follows:*
	Prince St. to Luckwell Rd.	*The application of the Bristol Tramways for 2 licences to operate*

the above service be acceded to, subject to the terminus being at the Luckwell Hotel, until such time that the remainder of Luckwell Rd. is completed to its junction with Winterstoke Rd.

Carey's Lane to Stapleton. Bristol Tramways, 2 licences subject to satisfactory arrangements being made with regard to James St., St. Werburghs.(Widening – author).

Prince St. and Brislington (Bloomfield Rd.). 2 licences for 3 months subject to arrangements at Skew Bridge (now known as New Bridge, Feeder Rd.) *and Wooton Rd.*

Carey's Lane and Wick Rd. Bristol Tramways, 2 additional licences granted.

Knowle & Ashton. Bristol Tramways, 2 licences, not acceded to.

Broad Plain & Raleigh Rd. Bristol Tramways. 3 licences not acceded to.

Avonmouth & Hotwells. Bristol Tramways to extend this service to Prince St. This was acceded to subject to satisfactory fares being arranged. (This joint service with Greyhound covered part of the Hotwells tram service and B. T. & C. C. wished to protect the tram fares on this section – Author).

Carey's Lane and Briar way. Bristol Tramways, 2 extra licences to provide a 10 minute service on either route.

Clyde Rd. and Bedminster. Bristol Tramways, one additional licence to operate between St. Augustines Parade & Sheane Rd. Not granted.

Carey's Lane to Eastville. Bristol Tramways requested 3 additional licences. Granted. The Eastville terminus to be altered to the centre of Robertson Rd.

Bristol (Prince St.) and Burnham on Sea. Bristol Tramways, 3 licences granted.

Bristol (Tramways Centre) and Weston Super Mare. Bristol Tramways, 2 additional licences granted.

Bristol (Tramways Centre) and Clevedon. Bristol Tramways, 2 additional licences granted.

The above two grants are subject to no vehicles standing outside the Sun building.

Bristol to Frampton Cotterell and Wotton-under-Edge. Bristol Tramways requested 2 licences to augment the service. Granted.

Bristol to Keynsham and Bath. Bristol Tramways requested to utilize the two licences granted to C.Russett for their Bristol to Keynsham service to augment the Bristol to Bath service. Granted.

Cheltenham and Weston Super Mare. Bristol Tramways asked for 4 licences. Granted, provided buses proceed to and from Prince St. via Cumberland Rd.

Bristol Tramways asked to extend the Colston St. – Suspension Bridge and Colston St. to Ashley Down Road to Temple Meads Station. Decision deferred.

Colston St. to Avonmouth or Filton service. Bristol Tramways applied to extend these services to Temple Meads. Not granted, but 4 licences to augment existing services granted.

Bristol (Prince St.) to Portishead. Bristol Tramways and Greyhound asked for 4 additional licences. Granted.

Bristol to Northampton. Greyhound granted 4 licences subject to 1/- minimum fare between Bristol and Bath.

Bristol to Weymouth. Greyhound granted 2 extra licences.

Bristol, Reading, London and Paignton. E. Jones (Morning Star) granted 2 spare licences.

Bristol, Salisbury, Southampton and Portsmouth. Olympic Motor Services Ltd. Of Portsmouth were granted 2 licences subject to starting from Prince St. and 1/- minimum fare being charged between Bristol and Bath.

Ashley Down, Sea Mills and Westbury. Bristol Tramways to operate this service to either side of Mill Pill Bridge (now undergoing reconstruction) *be acceded to. The Avonmouth service may also be so operated if such an application be made.*

Liverpool – Bristol. McShane Motors Ltd., Liverpool, application acceded to provided that they start by July 1st next.

21/5/30

E. Jones. 3 extra licences granted for use on the Bristol – London – Paignton service provided not more than seven vehicles are in use on any one day.

Greyhound and Birmingham & Midland Motor Omnibus C. Ltd.
Each granted 4 licences on their joint Bristol – Paignton – Plymouth service.

Gratton Bros., Burnham on Sea.
The Chief Constable wished to draw the attention of the sub-committee that he had recently been convicted of an indecent offence. No action to be taken.

16/6/30

Bristol Tramways. Prince St. to Ham Green, two extra licences granted 23/7/30.

Greyhound. It was agreed by them to fit pneumatic tyres to their double deckers at a meeting held on 23/7/30.

11/8/30

W. Ives. Bristol – Cirecncester service. Application to add one vehicle to this service, making two licences altogether. Granted 16/11/30.

Bristol Tramways and Greyhound.
Jointly to extend the Careys Lane to Filton Avenue service to Eden Grove. Filton Avenue will not be completed until December then one extra licence will be granted to each company. (Later delayed for three months.)

Watch (Traffic) Sub committee

9/7/30

Underwood Express Ltd.   Bristol to Portsmouth. 4 licences granted provided route is via Bath Rd., Bath Bridge, Clarence Rd., Commercial Rd., Wapping, Prince St. Bridge to Prince St. Local fares to or from Bristol and Bath to be 1/-.

Birmingham & Midland Motor Omnibus Co. Ltd.
Birmingham and Weston Super Mare service to operate via Southmead Rd., Henleaze Rd., Westbury Rd., Upper Belgrave Rd., Bridge Valley Rd., Hotwell Rd., Cumberland Basin Swing Bridge, Cumberland Rd., Wapping, Cumberland Rd. to Ashton Avenue.

Holt Bros.   Asked for 10 licences for their Rochdale to Torquay service to operate to and from 10, Broad Quay, not more than 2 journeys being made, vehicles to stand inside the garage at 10, Broad Quay.(Routes as B.&.M.M.O.C. above).

Empress Coaches of 15, Colston Avenue,
Asked to operate a 15 minute service from Colston Street to the new housing estate at Horfield. Not acceded to.

Elliot Bros. (Royal Blue.)
Bristol to Portsmouth. Licence granted subject to route and fares being set as for Olympic.

Archway Motor Coaches Ltd.
Requested 6 licences for Manchester – Bristol – Torquay or Ilfracombe. Granted subject to fares and routes as above.

Red & White.   Plymouth and South Wales via Bristol. Granted 6 licences, local routes and fares as above.

Greyhound.   Birmingham, Bristol and Plymouth. Applied for an additional licence to convey passengers direct to Clevedon.

Gratton Bros. Burnham on Sea.
2 licences for a Burnham on Sea to Bristol service. Not granted.

Bristol Tramways. Applied to move the Sneyd Park bus stop to the Downs side of Ivywell Rd. as an experiment.

3/12/30

McShanes Motorways, Liverpool.
Asked for 4 licences for a triangular service from Liverpool to Bristol and London.

Goughs garages Ltd. Asked for a Bristol – London licence.

Mr. Prescott raised the question of the old fashioned buses used by Bristol Tramways on the 21 service. It was resolved that the Chief Constable be authorized to approach Bristol Tramways on this subject.

7/1/31

G.A.Gough. One licence granted for his Bristol to London service for a new coach purchased by Mr. Gough.

2/2/31

Hackney licences to continue to 31/3/31:

Class "A" omnibuses:

B.T. & C.C.	222
Greyhound	66
Bath Tramways	3
E.Jones	11
Black & White	3
Gratton Bros.	2
Olympic	3
W.Ives	1
Elliot Bros. (Royal Blue).	68
Midland red	25

Class "B" charabancs	292
Total	696

8/7/31

Omnibus Station, Queen Square.

It is resolved that the west side of Queen Square behind Prince St. Omnibus Station to be used to park coaches.